How to Shoot Straight

Frontispiece A back view of the correct stance at the moment of firing at a tall bird to the left. The body is shaped like an extension of the stock behind the gun. Recoil is taken down the left leg. For a bird on the right, the weight is changed to the right leg. The left foot twists and lifts, like the right foot for the left-angled shot, as the bird is stroked out of the air. See FEET, *page 48 et seq.*

How to Shoot Straight

Macdonald Hastings

South Brunswick
New York: A. S. Barnes and Company

To the memory of

ROBERT CHURCHILL

To the American Hunter

When I was planning this manual my thought was that I should write a different version for the U.S.A., divesting my English cloth in the pictures for North American hunting gear; calling cartridges as you more appropriately call them, shells; swapping my London-best double-barrelled 12-bore game guns for a five-shot automatic.

Then it chanced that I was invited to shoot in a match with a team of U.S. army officers based in the United Kingdom. We Englishmen, all experienced game shots, took them on at skeet. Your boys took the pants off us. Next day, the party was invited to shoot again at driven pheasants. We took the pants off your lot. It is instructive, at the start of this drill book, to know the reason why.

The technique of skeet shooting is to "point-out" the target, vibrating the gun in readiness at the full length of the aiming arm, with the butt just clear of the shoulder, springing the gun on fire with a thrust of the shoulder on to the mark. It is a method which is ideally suited to dealing with inanimate targets, travelling at a known rate of speed, crossing at low angles in a limited field of fire.

It is a misleading introduction to shooting at live targets, coming unexpectedly from all angles and

9

travelling at a wide variation of range and pace.

We Englishmen, without the trick of it, lost at skeet. We were better in the field because, as I shall show you in the drill, "pointing-out" is hopeless when the way the target flies, and the m.p.h. it flies, is unpredictable.

It was the meeting with the American sportsmen, and the discussion we had later on shooting styles, which convinced me that it would be wrong to try and translate this book into an Englishman's "Americanese." Far better that you should see our school of shooting as it is.

This is English shooting grammar. I haven't dealt with rifle shooting, except for a note on the use of small bore shooting because Britain, apart from the stalking of red deer in the Highlands of Scotland, is scattergun country. I have deliberately limited the instructions to shooting on the wing, with only a word or two on ground game. The method I advocate, in its limited subject, is universal.

You will notice that, in my advice to European sportsmen, I am critical of pump guns, so popular on your side of the Atlantic. The fellows who beat us at skeet used them, but they were at a disadvantage with us in the field because they were lifting eight pounds while we were lifting six. We were swinging our guns that much quicker.

The U.S., I can't think why, has no proofing houses. The result is that American shotguns are made much heavier, for safety, than they need to be. For straight shooting, look for a light gun with a quick lift. The best shotguns in the world are still made in London (at a price!) and in Birmingham. If you can find the money, an English shotgun is incomparable. If you are able to acquire a London-best by one of the half-a-dozen top makers, you will have something which, in the world of shooting, is comparable to a Rembrandt.

But, whatever you shoot with and whatever you shoot

at, this book is designed to help you to shoot straighter.

Until the early years of the nineteenth century, straight shooting wasn't even practicable. Guns were inaccurate, powder was irregularly milled, and shot was soft. The most that people could achieve who went sporting in stove pipe hats was a cloud of black smoke out of which, possibly, they discovered, when the fog cleared, that they had killed an easy going-away bird sprung by a pointer or spaniel. For food for the larder, it was much easier to catch game by setting nets or wires.

It is generally conceded that the father of game-shooting on the wing was Colonel Peter Hawker, an English army officer who fought with Wellington in the Peninsular War, and who ultimately wrote a minor classic called *Instructions to Young Sportsmen.* Hawker's method, using a flint gun, was to ride down his quarry on horseback, point to point, until the game was so tired that it could hardly lift off the ground. Then he let off.

Nevertheless, Hawker, who lived long enough to exhibit his guns to Queen Victoria at the Great Exhibition in London in 1851, showed the way. With the development of breech loading weapons, modern shooting practice in Britain—driven game shooting—became possible. With that, it wasn't long before the sporting papers were competing to name, each year, "the ten best shots in England." A tradition of straight shooting was established, a tradition which I have endeavored to pass on to you in this book.

But there was an interval between the age of high shooting in England and a rational explanation of how it was practiced. None of the "ten best shots" appeared to be able to tell how they did it. What they wrote, those who wrote, is of no practical help at all. Indeed, the teaching, such as it was at the time, was blunderingly helpless.

It fell to Robert Churchill in this century to express

the logic of shooting at moving targets in grammatical terms. It fell to me to put his thoughts, and practice, into words.

Contents

Introducing the first principles of using a gun effectively and safety. The ability to shoot straight is not an inherited masculine gift. It is an art only to be acquired by practice and knowledge of the game.

Choose a gun, if you can afford it, to last a lifetime. If you can't afford a best gun, learn how to choose a second-hand one. The most successful modern game gun is the 12-bore. Buying a used arm, make sure it is proofed for smokeless cartridges; that the barrels are not unduly pitted, or dented; and that the action is sweet. Chose a gun to fit as carefully as a new suit.

An explanation of the basic rules of handling firearms safely. If in doubt, don't shoot. Never be ashamed to be caught with an empty gun. Never carry a gun at the trail. The most natural method of carrying a gun, in the "shoulder arms" position, is not necessarily the safest.

13

Contents 15

A final reminder, with a note on the sort of mistakes officialdom makes, that the man who thinks that the ability to shoot will come naturally is a dangerous fool. Good shots are made, not born.

List of Illustrations

Frontispiece

Emphasizing the basic principle that the gun—in this picture taking a tall pheasant—is an extension of the body of the man using it. The photos, between pages 54-55, show how the technique is applied to shots at lower angles.

Between pages 26-27

Use your own feet, hands and gun to familiarize yourself with the lessons illustrated here. Knowing how *not* to put your feet, how *not* to hold your gun, is just as important as knowing the right way of doing it.

Between pages 54-55

On either side of the middle spread of photographs, the positions shown are rest positions. They should be practiced to exercise arm muscles, and to increase familiarity with the feel of the gun. Half the art of straight shooting, perhaps more, starts from a correct gun-carrying position. The shooting poses in the middle are frozen at the instant of trigger pressure to demonstrate how, at varying angles, the whole body moves after the gun. The body, and eyes, are instinctively aiming the barrels.

Between pages 82-83

Know the weapon you are using. It is just as important as understanding how to aim it. People who drive cars, with the boast that they don't know what goes on under the bonnet, are not the best drivers. People who use guns, without a knowledge of the rules of proof and the comparatively simple mechanism, are seldom the straight safe shots.

Between pages 108-109

The four basic models of shotgun you are likely to handle, or see (apart from single-barrelled weapons or repeating arms). You should recognize them at a glance.

How to Shoot Straight

1

First Round

It is masculine weakness to imagine that guns are things that every proper man should know how to handle as a sort of birthright. The Wild West legend, of the quick draw and characters who could cut the pip out of an Ace of Spades, has done a dangerous lot to encourage it. Nevertheless, he is an odd sort of man who is not fascinated by the wicked glint of a gun.

The danger, it's a very real one, is that a man who plays with any sort of arm, without a proper knowledge of its correct use and lethal power, is risking his own life, and other people's. The safest object when a novice is wielding a gun is the one he is aiming to hit. Those is most danger are the people who are with him.

The purpose of this text book is to teach correct gun handling in the presence of others (they're usually there) and to school the reader in the technique of straight safe shooting. It isn't easily acquired.

The best way is to have it kicked into you, under field conditions, from your early teens; to be sent home, for example if, when you are reloading, you raise your barrel to the stock instead of the stock to a lowered barrel. The next best way is to go to a shooting school and be coached in the art of breaking clays. But it's an expensive game; and, since the flight of the clay is

21

predictable, it's not quite the same thing as shooting in the field.

A first class shooting coach, giving you personal instruction, will teach you far more quickly than I can in a book. But few are lucky enough to be able to afford that sort of training. This is next best. If you study what I tell you, you shouldn't be at a disadvantage in the most critical company.

This manual is based on what I was taught by Robert Churchill, the great sporting gunmaker to whose memory I have dedicated it. In collaboration with Churchill, I wrote *Churchill on Gameshooting,** which explains his method. But I have felt for a long time that Churchill's book, addressed to the well-to-do, is not the first book for the man who has to count the value of every cartridge, and choose the guns he buys to fit his pocket.

This is for the ordinary chap. My aim is to teach you what Churchill taught me; what I have learnt by trial and error myself; and, above all, to show you how you can achieve the enviable reputation of being known as a reliable shot.

Accurate gunmanship, with a shotgun or a rifle, is an accomplishment as difficult to acquire as a low handicap at golf. Everybody knows that you can't achieve competence with a golf club without constant practice and a knowledge of the game. Yet shooting men complain, after no practice at all, that they are out of form. In the current phrase, it's "not on." You have to work at it.

The difference between shooting and ball games is that in shooting youth and quick sight is not a primary consideration. Some of the very best shots are elderly men who simply know how to use their feet, their arms, their heads and their guns.

I have endeavored in this textbook to discuss the various sporting quarries of the world. I have placed the

* *Churchill on Gameshooting,* a completely revised edition by Macdonald Hastings, 1963 (Michael Joseph).

emphasis not on rifle shooting but on shotgun work. I have limited my comments on rifles to small bore weapons. The reason is that, for the average sportsman, the shotgun is the most common arm. It also happens that it is the one which, in the field, is the most challenging to use successfully.

In large game shooting, no good sportsman should draw a bead unless he is sure. The game is the stalk, and, in the hunting of dangerous animals, the moment of truth is a test rather of nerve than of sheer marksmanship. When a big game hunter has the worst of an encounter, the explanation is almost certainly that he panicked, mishandled the bolt when he tried to slip a new round into the chamber of his rifle. With the chances ninety per cent in his favor, he shouldn't have muffed it.

In shotgun shooting, where there is no danger from the game, there is a deeper responsibility for the man behind the gun. In humanity, he must know his business. I've tried to show you here how to learn it.

2

How to Choose a Shotgun *

A new gun isn't necessarily a good gun. An old gun isn't necessarily a bad one. If you have to choose between an old bad gun and a cheap new one, then go for the new one.

The disadvantage of cheap new guns is that they are made to last. They may look all right in the gunshop, with freshly blued barrels and scrolls of gingerbread on the lock-plates; but the action is usually blacksmithed together so roughly that you have to have a finger like a traction engine to pull the trigger.

If you buy a cheap gun you are sooner or later buying defects which will show in shot out barrels after a few thousand rounds, and faults in the action which may well prove beyond repair. However carefully you try to nurse it, your gun, as soon as the varnish wears off, will look the gaspipe it is. That's no reflection on the manufacturers. The reflection is in the price. You can't buy a good gun, a gun which handles sweetly and lasts, for peanuts.

Go for a gun, and plunge as deeply into your pocket as you can afford, which will last your whole lifetime, and perhaps your son's as well. I am not suggesting what you should pay. Sufficient that the more you pay the more certain it is that your gun, if you look after it properly, will increase in value as the years go by.

* Because it is a far simpler to choose small bore rifles, I have dealt with them in a separate chapter.

For example a best London gun, the most beautifully built shotgun in the world, cost, before the Kaiser's war, sixty guineas. Between the Kaiser's and Hitler's wars, the price rose to one hundred and twenty guineas. Today, the price for a new gun is round about a thousand pounds. Guns made in London half a century ago have a second-hand value now far in excess of their original price. They are guns built by craftsmen to fire a hundred thousand rounds, and like it for a hundred thousand more.

If you choose a medium priced gun, somewhere between the cheapest mass-produced arm and the tremendously expensive hand-made guns of which a few are still produced in London, it is likely to be what is called a pump gun, a coventional side-by-side double-barrelled weapon, a single—barrelled arm or an over-and-under.

These guns are well made, and shoot just as straight and as far, at a tenth of the price, as the guns made by the great hand craftsmen. The difference is in weight, and in the subtler difference between a tailor-measured suit and clothes off the peg.

Medium priced new guns are generally heavier, and longer in the barrels, than top priced ones. Half-a-pound extra can make a little difference a big difference after a long day in the field. Young men don't notice it; older men do.

So my advice, here at the start, is that you don't buy the cheapest gun you can find, which will be worthless in a year or two. A medium-priced gun—I recommend it to a young man with a limited pocket—can be traded against a better gun in the years ahead. But, in my heart, I believe that the best way to begin is with a second-hand one.

The best place to buy a second-hand gun is from a gunmaker. Gunmakers usually have a large stock. You will probably pay more; but you will have the comfort of knowing that the gunmaker, with his own reputation to consider, has seen to it that the weapon has been properly regulated, proofed for smokeless powders, and can be regarded as safe.

Alternatively, you can buy from another fellow by private treaty. You will buy, generally speaking, more cheaply; but, unless you know what you are about, more uncertainly. You can reduce the risk if, when somebody has made you an offer, you know what to look for.

The priority is to break the gun into its three component parts, and to examine the marks stamped on the flats in the base of the barrels (*see plates between pages* 82-83). If it is an English gun, the marks on guns proofed abroad are different; you should find a device incorporating the letters NP or BNP, and/or the words NITRO PROOF. That means that the weapon has been passed by the Proof House in London or in Birmingham as safe for use with modern smokeless powders. It has been subjected to a proof charge well in excess of the pressures developed by modern standard cartridges.

If the letters NP are not present among the provisional and definitive proof marks DON'T buy the gun,* however well preserved it seems, and however cheap it is. It means that the weapon is almost certainly over sixty years old. If you fire modern cartridges with it, it is liable to disintegrate in your hand.

Even if the gun carries nitro-proof marks, *and it is an old gun*, you must beware. The marks do not guarantee that the gun is *still* "in proof." At some time in its life, the barrels could have been bored or lapped-out to remove "pitting," a state of affairs induced by corrosion. In that event, it may well be that the bore has been enlarged beyond the limit at which it was proofed. That's another good reason, if you are buying a second-hand gun, for getting it from a reputable

---

* Unless, of course, you are a collector; or intend to use it with BLACK POWDER only. See page 112 *et seq.*

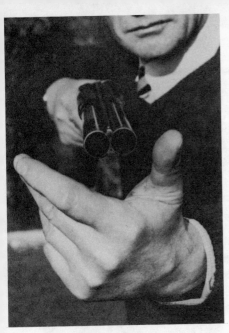
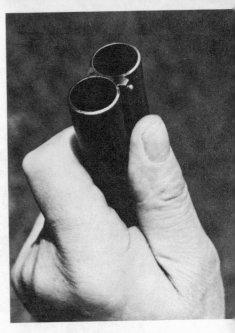

FIRST PRINCIPLES: Your left hand is your aiming hand. The barrels of your gun will point where the cup between your thumb and forefinger swings it. If you see the brass bead of your foresight, when you shoot at a moving target, you will miss. Your right hand is simply a lifting and trigger-pressing hand. You will miss if your stance is not squarely balanced in readiness for a smooth body movement.

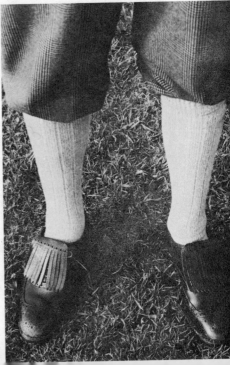

WRONG: Your stance is too narrow. You will be off-balance, and catch recoil, when you fire.

WRONG: The "aggressive" stance with left foot too far forward, usually accompanied by a flinching shoulder.

WRONG: Feet splayed too wide. The gun will punish you standing like this. You have no freedom of movement.

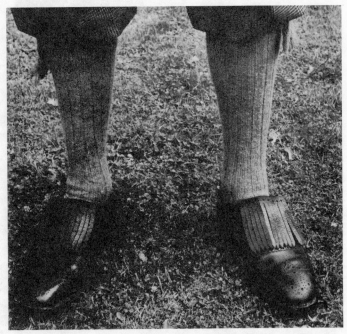

RIGHT: You are poised square on target, ready to turn your heels 90 degrees in any direction.

WRONG: The "natural" way of carrying a gun at the walk is the dangerous way. With every step, the barrels are swinging into the line of the man who is probably walking beside you. Even if you believe that you are alone, the fact is that, in this crowded country, you are never alone.

RIGHT: The "unnatural" way is the right way. As you walk, push your gun across your chest so that the barrels are pointing straight in front of you. It is good practice to cant the barrels slightly upwards. You will find that, when the chance shows of a shot, you come much more fluently and accurately on to the mark.

gunmaker; or, at any rate, getting it checked by one. Second-hand guns, they are often tenth-hand guns, can be as full of hidden flaws as second-hand cars.

Having satisfied yourself that the gun is still proofed for smokeless cartridges, look down the barrels into the light from both ends. If it's an old gun, or a gun which hasn't been looked after properly, the metal will almost certainly be pitted. This is not necessarily a dissuader, although it marks a reduction in the value.

If the pitting isn't too bad, study the barrels themselves for *dents*. Dents are more damaging than pitting because, every time a shot is fired, pressure is applied to the weakest part of the metal. Most old guns, which haven't had the attention of a skilled gunmaker, carry dents. If it's not too late, they can be raised. But you will have to pay to have the service done.

Next, assemble the gun and hold it up to the light. If you can see light between the barrels and the face of the action it needs tightening by a gunmaker. The chambers of a good gun shouldn't close properly on the action face if there is as much as a piece of paper in between.

Try the trigger pulls with snap caps *(described on page 122)* or empty cartridge cases in the breech. The pull on a service rifle is seven and a half pounds. The pull of a shotgun should be about three and a half pounds. In old guns, with swollen wood and rusty actions, it can be as much as fifteen pounds. If you have to make an effort to release the action, you may be certain that the gun is in a mess inside.

People who want to sell you guns, even people whose guns are not for sale, will inevitably tell you that theirs is the hardest-hitting gun they've ever known. Don't believe a word of it. A gun is only as effective as the propellant in the breech. Barrels, choked at the muzzle ends, hold a charge together closer than a cylinder. The shot from the cartridge doesn't travel further, but in a tighter pack. If you shoot very straight, that's useful. But most old guns, although they may still have a future, have long ago had the constriction of metal about the barrels shot clean out of them. Old guns have tubes which are paper thin.

It would be less than fair if I didn't confess that I have known many men who have regularly, and efficiently, used guns which, theoretically, ought to have blown up on them. Unbelievably, I have seen weapons braced with wire, pitted in the barrels like colanders, proofed only for black powder, pulling down tall pheasants. I would be less than truthful if I didn't admit that I have taken chances myself.

But don't do it. Luck runs out. I have come to the conclusion that there's a risk in the use of lethal weapons which is unavoidable. But it is a responsibility to reduce it to a minimum. When you choose a gun, start straight.

Now consider, not the quality, but the sort of shotgun that you want.

You have the choice of a pump gun, holding five cartridges with rifle-type action or a boxlock or a sidelock, the types of action most widely favored by European sportsmen. Pump guns are not generally welcome in the British shooting field. There is an unfounded prejudice that they are unfair. I don't agree with that. My own criticism is that pump guns are barrel-heavy. I prefer a double-barrelled English gun, for speed and quick handling, every time.

Your own choice is likely to be between a box and a sidelock, (illustrated opposite page 108). You can recognize the difference at a glance because a sidelock has a lozenged-shaped lock plate which extends in a graceful curve over the trigger guard. The action of the boxlock is cut off square. The sidelock is the traditional lock which was used on the old hammer guns. It is still the lock which is used in the most expensive sporting guns today. It *looks* better, and it is better.

Nevertheless, the sidelock is not more reliable than the boxlock, a simple mechanism with only three moving parts evolved by two Birmingham craftsmen at the turn of the century named Anson and Deeley. As a consequence, boxlocks are still sometimes known as "A & D's."

If money is no object, a good sidelock is aesthetically the most beautiful weapon you can have. But, whatever you do, don't buy a *cheap* sidelock. You are buying trouble. A boxlock is what you want for sturdy pedestrian service. It is even more important to use a boxlock shotgun in those parts of the world where a skilled repair service isn't readily available.

Guns without an ejector mechanism to spring clear spent cartridges can be bought much more cheaply than ejector-fitted weapons. If price is the main consideration, your shooting will be none the worse if you have to finger out the spent cartridges from the chambers. But reloading will be slower. In the end, you will regret that you didn't invest in the first place in a self-ejector gun.

The most popular size of game shooting gun today is called a 12-bore. It is an arbitrary term. What was called a 14-bore in the days of muzzle-loading guns is called a 12-bore today.

You can shoot with a .410, based on a mathematical calculation of the diameter of the barrel (I am sorry that it is so confusing, but I didn't invent the system); and you can choose a 20-bore, a 16-bore or even a 10- or 8-bore. Other gauges are available, but forget them. They are not normally made.

There is a theory that the first gun that a boy should be allowed to handle is a .410, the smallest calibre which can be effectively employed against flying targets. A .410

has the merit of not having an appreciable kick; it is light
in weight and, although it fires only about half the shot
charge in a standard 12-bore cartridge, it is just as lethal
if the charge is well directed. No doubt, the .410 has a
place for the destruction of rats; and a place, too, for
the uses of poachers and criminals. As for me, *I* know so
much about the horrible things that have been
perpetrated by .410's, especially the folding sort, that I
would not give them house room.

A 20-bore is possibly the best gauge of gun to start
using on a shooting career. The kick is negligible; the
performance in the hands of a good shot is first class.
The danger is the keeping of 20-bores and 12-bores in
the same house. A 20-bore cartridge will lodge in the end
of the chamber of a 12-bore. If a 12-bore cartridge is
loaded behind it, the result will be a burst barrel.

In England 16-bores are eclectics' guns and some of
the most magnificent shots use them in order to save weight.
The snag, briefly, is that if you run out of blue 16-bore
cartridges (they're normally blue) you can seldom
borrow from your neighbor. But they are more widely
used on the continent.

The wildflower's guns, the 10's and the 8's, are
increasingly going out of fashion. They kick like mules,
the cartridges cost the earth, and because of their weight,
they are so slow to handle that a man with a 12-bore
can gain yards on them, cancelling out the increased
range of the heavier gun. The ideal gun for a wildflower
these days is a 12-bore chambered for 3-inch cartridges.

The 12-bore is the weapon today. If you are a very
good shot, you can afford to have full choke in both
barrels. If you are an average shot, look for improved
cylinder in the right, and half-choke in the left. Simply,
this means that the column of shot out of the cartridge
is steadied, as it goes out the gun, into a narrow, or less
narrow pattern. It is better, unless you happen to be one

of those people who fires the back trigger of your gun first, to have the closer pattern in the left barrel. At close ranges, which shots with the right barrel usually are, it is better to have the more open pattern. At longer ranges, when you have missed with the right, the tighter pattern will make up for the increase in distance between gun and target.

So that you know what the performance of your gun should be—you shouldn't buy a second-hand gun without testing it—here is a table, based on a 12-bore gun with a standard cartridge, to guide you. You can experiment by firing at sheets of newspaper.

Super choke should put 75 per cent or 225 pellets out of a 300 pellet charge within a 30 inch circle at 40 yards.

Full choke should put 70 per cent or 210 pellets within a 30 inch circle at 40 yards.

Three-quarter choke should put 65 per cent or 195 pellets within a 30 inch circle at 40 yards.

Half choke should put 60 per cent or 180 pellets within a 30 inch circle at 40 yards.

Quarter choke, better known as Improved Cylinder, should put 50 per cent or 150 pellets into a 30 inch circle at 40 yards.

One-eighth choke should put 45 per cent or 135 pellets into a 30 inch circle at 40 yards.

True Cylinder should put 40 per cent or 120 pellets into a 30 inch circle at 40 yards.

From that don't jump to the conclusion that super choke is the best for you. It most certainly isn't. Nearly all shots at game are well within the range of improved cylinder. With a looser pattern you will have a better chance of hitting the target.

The most favored barrel length for a shotgun today is 28 inches. Up to the end of the nineteenth century, guns with 30-inch barrels, and more, were fashionable. In our century, guns with 25-inch barrels are widely used. The 30-inch barrel suited the slower burning black powder, before nitro powder was introduced. Someone once said, probably facetiously, "the longer the barrels the nearer the bird!"

The theory was a fallacious one. It overlooked the fact takes longer to lift a 30-inch barrel than a shorter one. The 25-inch gun, Robert Churchill's speciality, owing to its shorter length, comes up quicker, and is lighter to handle. The argument against 25-inch guns is that there is a loss in velocity—it happens that it's a negligible loss—and the kick is perhaps fractionally sharper than the heavier gun with a longer barrel. Although I have shot with Churchill short-barrelled guns all my life, I am now inclined to the view that they are more suitable for a short square-shouldered man than a tall thin one.

Guns with barrels longer than 30 inches are now obsolete, and guns with barrels below 25 inches make an uncomfortable crack when they are fired. They are suitable only for gangsters. It is important to add that, unless the weapon happens to be one of the very rare ones these days—a true cylinder—long gun barrels cannot be shortened without a loss of efficiency. The reason is that the removal of the choke, the thickening of metal at the muzzle ends, means the removal of the control which ensures that the gun fires a regular pattern.

If you are lucky enough to have a gun measured and built for you, the gunmaker will see to it that it fits; and that the shape of the stock and the trigger guard suits you like a well made suit of clothes. My notion is that most people who read this handbook won't be able to afford luxuries like that. If you buy from a reputable gunmaker, he will help you; probably modify the bend and the length of the stock, without extra cost, to bring the gun into line with your own sight and figure.

But I'll assume that you haven't got a gunmaker to

help you. (1) The first rough and ready check to establish whether the length of the stock suits is to press the butt of the gun into the crook of your arm and test whether the pad of your finger reaches comfortably over the guard. If you've got a length of finger to spare, the stock is too short for you. If you have difficulty in reaching the trigger, the stock is too long. Stocks can be cut down, or increased in length, relatively cheaply. (2) Making sure that your gun is empty, ask a friend to act as a marker for you. Show him that the gun is empty too. Ask him to hold up an index finger. The range needn't be more than ten yards. If your friend assures you that you are on the mark, the gun is a fair fit. If you look to the left or right, the stock requires bending one way or the other to bring you naturally on the mark.

If you are using a borrowed gun, or you haven't got the means or the opportunity to have your own gun altered, you can, to a certain degree, *fit yourself to your gun* by regulating your grip. If the stock is too long, draw your hand if necessary right up the barrels. King George V, one of the greatest game shots of his day, always used what is known as the long armed stance, stretching his left hand forward during gun mounting until his left arm was fully extended up the barrels when he fired.

If you are off target with both eyes open—check yourself by firing into double spread sheets of newspaper—check the result when you shoot with one eye closed. Churchill always opposed this practice. But it is the right solution for the man who has got to fit himself to an ill-fitting gun.

Young men find it easier to adapt themselves to guns that are not made for them than older ones. To shoot well, a mature man has a greater need for a gun which is a good fit.

Make checks for fit on a double-spread of newspaper

with a big black ink mark in the center of your point of aim. Shoot from a measured sixteen yards, and watch your mean average. The object of the exercise is to make sure whether it is you, or the gunfit, which is at fault. The position of the pattern of shot on the target will tell you.*

You Are Shooting To The Right of The Ink Mark:

Causes may be: (a) that the cast of the stock is too great for you; (b) your head is too far forward and your eyes too far over the stock; (c) the stock is too short; (d) you are adopting an incorrect stance.

You Are Shooting Left Of The Ink Mark:

Causes may be: (a) The cast of the stock is too straight for you; (b) The stock is too long; (c) you are reducing the length of the gun by pulling in your left hand; (d) you are putting the butt into your arm instead of thrusting your shoulder into it.

You Are Shooting Low:

Causes may be: (a) The bend of the stock is too much for you; (b) the trigger pull is too heavy; (c) you are flinching; (d) your aiming is not far enough forward or, alternatively, your gun is barrel heavy and, consequently, is sinking on fire.

You Are Shooting High:

Causes may be: (a) The stock is too straight for you; (b) the trigger pull—unlikely, but possible—is too light; (c)

---

* You will be better able to make the practical tests suggested here after studying the rest of this instruction manual.

your stock is too long for your arms.

To make a simple experiment to test whether the length of stock on your gun suits you, the overhead shot is the best. For the going-away shot, whatever the size of the gun, you can extend or shorten the reach of the left hand to make the gun fit. But in the overhead shot, if the gun doesn't fit really well, you will recognize that something is wrong. If the stock is too long, you may well find that your swing is checked. You may indeed discover that you can shoot more easily by using the second trigger. If the stock is too short, you will notice that you have to push your left hand up the barrel to make a smooth and natural follow-through.

If the stock is finally proved to be at fault, it should be altered by an expert who has seen you shoot. Self-gun-fitting is very much like self-doctoring; not by any means a certain cure. Nevertheless, to suspect a malady is the first step in locating it, and putting yourself in the way of a cure.

3

How to be Safe with a Gun

Let me frighten you. A shotgun at short range, even a small bored gun like a .410, is so terrifyingly lethal that it will carve a good size hole in mud. Think that at ranges, of say 60 to 80 yards, a single pellet in the leg is comparable to being swiped with a cricket bat on the calf. A gunshot, apparently correctly aimed, can ricochet off a flint, and destroy the eye of a man standing out of the line of it. It has happened.

You should not be carrying a gun at all unless you have insured yourself against accident. Even if the accident is not your own fault in criminal law, in civil law you are responsible. You can safeguard yourself by taking out a comprehensive sportsman's insurance policy. Alternatively, if you don't want to cover yourself, you can take out a third party insurance just in case—perhaps through no fault of yours—you can damage somebody else. The rates charged are very reasonable.

Now I'm going to give you three commandments in the hope that you don't break the original sixth. I'm sure you know the basic rules about never pointing a gun at anyone; one must always assume the gun is loaded; that accidents happen, often out of the most improbable circumstances.

No gun is ever safe; nor in its nature could it be.

Unfortunately, it has become the custom among gunmakers to engrave the word "SAFE" when a catch inside the action has been engaged on the trigger. It isn't safe. The sears and tumblers of the action are *never* locked.

The best word you could use for it is "CHECK," because there are ways in which the actions of even the best of guns can be jarred off against a slide set on "SAFE." Again and again, accidents have happened through people relying on that fatal word. Don't. It simply means that, if the gun is in good working order, it is less likely to go off by accident than otherwise. It isn't safe, any more than if you pass a green light on a traffic sign without checking that the automatic mechanism is in order.

Every time you handle a loaded gun remind yourself of the hazard—I've come to think there is an irreducible minimum for even the most careful shot—of accident.

I'm not preaching to you as somebody who is "holier than thou." Rather, I am a sinner who has committed most mistakes without, mercifully, doing anybody any harm. I want to show you, out of my own experience, how to avoid repeating errors that I have made myself.

Please treat these commandments which follow very, very seriously. They are longer than the biblical ones; but the shooting man who obeys them conscientiously will be asked by his friends to shoot again the next time, and the next.

DON'T TRUST ANY GUN. If you forget safety for a moment, that will be the moment in which something could happen which you will regret for the rest of your life.

IF IN DOUBT, DON'T SHOOT. No target is worth taking a chance for. Never pull the trigger unless you are quite sure that no one, even someone you couldn't reasonably expect to be there, might be in the line of fire.

DON'T BE ASHAMED TO CARRY AN EMPTY GUN. It is admittedly exasperating to be caught with an empty gun when a chance offers, perhaps the one chance in a day in the field, of killing a pheasant. Far better that way than a wild and ill-considered shot which might come off nine hundred and ninety nine times out of a thousand. It's the thousand to one chance that you must always think about.

I recognize that these commandments appear like a spoil sport start to a book on straight shooting. They are not because, if you get into a fixed habit of safe gun handling, you can enjoy your sport without the nagging fear of regret.

Here are the habits I am anxious for you to cultivate:

(1) Theoretically, the safest way to carry a gun is over the shoulder, with the muzzles pointing skywards. A shotgun should be held in the shoulder-arms position with the trigger-guard upwards. In practice, it is probably safer to carry the gun in the crook of the arm with the muzzles pointing into the ground. The most experienced shots carry guns that way.

You will gain points from your friends if you carry your gun, when you are not shooting, broken under your arm. Your friends will then be able to see for themselves that the chambers are empty and safe. Incidentally, you will find that a broken gun carries more lightly.

Never, never carry a gun at the trail.

It will be evident that pump guns and small bore rifles are weapons in which there is generally no outward show of what is in the breech. They are consequently rather more dangerous. (2) The game is shooting, whatever you shoot at. So most of the time you will be holding a loaded gun. If you are in company waiting for a shot, never lay your gun across your chest or across your knees. In that position, you are pointing your gun at someone on your left or right. If your stance is a semi-ready one, press the butt plate of the gun into your thigh with muzzles pressing forward, and upwards, across your body to the front. If you are in a sitting position, rest the butt of your gun on your thigh with barrels held skywards. In that pose you are safe, and ready for quick mounting. In more leisurely moments take the loaded gun under the crook of your arm, pointing safely into the ground in front of you. If you are alone—after pigeons, for example—you must never assume that you are really alone. I remember a case in which a man took a blind shot at an unexpected rabbit in a wood to discover that, only by the grace of God, he hadn't peppered a loving couple who had crept in among the brambles.

(3) In company, especially when people are walking in line, it is vital that guns be carried according to the rules. The natural way to carry a gun is across the chest. The result is that with every pace you are swinging your gun across your neighbor's body.

The only proper way to carry a gun at the walk is, oddly enough, an unnatural one. The left hand should be used to press the barrels of the gun into a forward position.*

In due course, I will show you that, if you hold your gun this way in the Ready Position, you are more likely to shoot what you are looking at.

Repeat: WALKING UP. PUSH YOUR GUN AWAY FROM YOUR CHEST SO THAT IT IS POINTING IN FRONT OF YOU.

(4) A high proportion of gun accidents are caused by people crossing stiles, fences, plank bridges and, in particular. wire without emptying their guns. NEVER PUSH THROUGH SO MUCH AS A HEDGEROW WITHOUT TAKING OUT THE CARTRIDGES.

---

* Throughout the book, a left-handed man should obviously reverse the instructions.

In company, when guns are being used from hand to hand over an obstruction, I have noticed that shooting men are usually careful. The people who have been found shot dead, often gamekeepers, have usually been alone. They just didn't bother to empty their guns when they slung their legs over a bit of barbed wire they had crossed so many times before. They did it once too often.

WHEN YOU ARE ALONE BE DOUBLY CAREFUL FOR YOUR OWN SAKE.

(5) When you are shooting fur, watch the nature of the ground; a charge of lead shot can ricochet in the most incredible manner. Most experienced shots, when they are out with a partner, refrain from shooting any fur in front. They only shoot when the hare, it is usually a hare these days, has crossed the line and is bolting away behind. The rule can be violated, but you need to have a lot of experience to make the exceptions. If in doubt, however anxious you are to have a shot, hold your gun up. There is always another time, another hare.

(6) Never pick up another man's gun without asking whether you can look at it, or without assuring yourself that he is as careful with the safety of his own weapon as you, I hope, are with yours.

Churchill, when he was displaying a gun, even in his own shop, made a practice of opening the barrels, showing the chambers, and saying "EMPTY" before he put the gun in your hands. You couldn't do better than to emulate his example yourself.

(7) Double check that your gun is unloaded every time that you put it in a car. A loaded gun in a car is a murderer. I have a recent memory of a young man who blew his stomach out pulling a loaded .410 by the muzzle from the back seat. If you have got a gun in the car, and you know that it is unloaded, still take the trouble of lifting it out from the butt end. The rule is that guns are always loaded.

(8) Never keep a loaded gun in the house. People do this so that they will be ready for a quick shot out of the window at a grey squirrel, or predators in the garden. What happens is that some trigger-happy visitor pulls the trigger.

(9) Make the habit, at the start of your shooting career, of breaking the gun, and looking down the barrels at the beginning of a shooting day; and at regular intervals during it. This is especially important if you are wildfowling; if there is snow and when the ground is muddy and the weather wet. Note that experienced shots have a way of blowing up the barrels of their guns. There is no merit in the puff of breath through the barrels. It is simply a way of concentrating attention that all's clear. Modern guns, which are relatively safe from mechanical and metal failure, cease to be safe if there is a blockage, such as mud or snow in the barrels. Blowing through the tubes, checking clear daylight before you settle to shoot, is a good habit.

(10) Oddly enough, modern smokeless cartridges, outside the chambers of the gun, are not particularly dangerous. I don't recommend it, on grounds of expense, but you can throw a smokeless cartridge on the fire, and it will ignite with little more than a harmless pop. Black powder, not used in modern cartridges, is on the contrary very dangerous. I have discussed black powder in the chapter on muzzle loading guns (Page 112).

Some men, who ought to know better, make a practice of hotting up their cartridges on the kitchen stove before the day's shooting. It increases the explosive pressure; but it is questionable whether it kills one bird the more. It is not to be recommended. Although there is no evidence to the contrary, it could be dangerous.

It is salutory to record that there was a case, at a shooting party on Lord Cadogan's Estate at Culford, in East Anglia, in the winter of 1922, in which fifteen cartridges in a man's pocket blew up with a "whizzing noise" and "a huge flash." The man fell dying with a gaping wound in his groin. The accident has never been explained. It was calculated that the odds against it happening were one thousand million to one, multiplied by all the years since the modern "safety cartridge" was developed.

It just shows how careful you need to be.

Repeat: NO GUN IS COMPLETELY SAFE. AND NO CARTRIDGE EITHER.

After this admonitory chapter—it is essential that you should be warned first—let's enjoy ourselves.

4

The Churchill Shooting School

Every shotgun has a bead over the muzzles of the barrels which is defined as the foresight. Anybody who uses the foresight to aim at a moving target will, unless he flukes, miss. There is a reason why. A shotgun is a weapon of movement. If you halt the gun to align the sights you will inevitably shoot behind the target.

A rifle, by contrast, is a weapon of immobility in which it is vital to balance the head of the foresight of the U of the backsight. For that reason *it is unusual for a man to be a first class rifle shot and a first class expert with a game gun at the same time*. The two styles are contradictory. Don't try to be the universal shot all at once.

Once upon a time, the custom was to teach sportsmen to draw a bead with a shotgun. The theory was that you calculated varying "forward allowances" according to the speed and angle of the target. It was an appallingly complicated way of teaching shotgun work. It meant that the shooter had to make a rapid calculation of the speed and distance of the target, with allowance for the time lag in trigger-pulling and the action of the lock mechanism on the primer of the cartridge. Assuming the estimated speed of his quarry was 30 m.p.h., he was supposed to allow 2½ feet at 20 yards, 4 feet at 30 yards, and 6 feet at 40 yards. The odds on the shooter getting the speed of the target right, the distance right, and timing his own reaction, were about as long as finding the treble chance on the football pools.

Although shooting was taught like that, people who performed well with a shotgun, forgot "forward allowance." Otherwise, they couldn't have shot as well as they did. But, significantly, none of them gave a rational explanation of how they achieved the result. It fell to Robert Churchill to pioneer a new method of teaching to shoot straight. It is the method I am expounding.

Dismissing the traditional theory that the way to shoot at a moving target is to place your gun to intercept it in the air, he taught that the first principle is the first principle of golf, or any ball game: Keep your eye on the target. If your eye wanders to the extent that you see your gun barrels—worst of all the foresight on the end—or your attention lapses just enough so that you hear your gun go off, you have missed.

The secret of shotgun work, Churchill taught, is to forget all about "forward allowance" and rely on your eyes, combined with a smooth swing and balanced body movement, to make the necessary allowance for you. *The eye is never wrong.*

Just knowing that is only a beginning to the art of straight shooting. You will still miss if you try too hard, hang on to the trigger; or make a fault of style with hands, feet, or head. You will never be a consistent shot until, having mastered the drill, you have acquired *muscle memory.*

When you go for a walk or a swim, you don't have to think to yourself how to do it. But as a baby you had to learn to walk; and most of us can remember how we floundered about when we were learning to swim. You have to learn how to shoot. Once learned you don't have to think how you do it any more. Muscle memory asserts itself.

When you miss, you will know why you missed. With practice you will even learn where you miss. You will settle down, perhaps not as a great shot, but as a consistent one.

In time, as cricketers do, you will develop your own style. But you must begin by learning how to play with a straight bat.

For the present, follow the instructions in the drill section, in the next chapter, as if you were on the parade ground, and I were the sergeant-major. The difference is that, unlike the sergeant-major, I have endeavored to explain why you should do as I tell you.

Ideally, you should study the drill with this book on the table, and the gun—an empty one!—at your side for dry practice. At this stage, you are not to pull the triggers. Indeed, you should never pull the triggers of an empty shotgun. The release of the triggers jars the action. If you must pull the triggers, load the chambers with metal snapcaps, which you can get at any gun shop.

5

Drill

Your gun, if you hope to be a sound shot, should become an extension of yourself. Another name for a gun is an arm. You must practice so that you handle your arm as rhythmically for its purpose as your own arms, legs, and head. If your limbs are not moving rhythmically with the gun, you might just as well be letting off fireworks.

It follows that, if you have a gun which you think fits you and suits you, it is inadvisable to chop and change. However much you experiment—and experimenting is certainly fun—you will always shoot best with a gun you believe in. I myself have experimented with different sorts of guns, more than most; but, when I am off form, I can usually bring myself on target again by shooting with the first good gun I ever owned. I know that all I am doing now is giving myself a psychological lift; but, in shooting, a familiar gun is like a lucky pair of old boots to a footballer.

Concentrate on THE DRILL. When you have established *muscle memory*, you will be a far wiser judge whether the gun is wrong, or you.

(1) PICK UP YOUR GUN: Not any old way. Lift it by the small of the stock, the forehand, or both.* Never lift a gun by the muzzle-ends. Apart from being a dangerous practice it is a giveaway of inexperience which sportsmen

*For the parts of a shotgun see page facing 83.

notice in the way that a horseman, horses too, can spot a novice by the way he gathers the reins.

Holding the gun by the small of the stock in your right hand (*reverse throughout for left-handers*), lay your index finger in an extended position along the trigger-guard. Don't touch the triggers. You are, in effect, using your index finger as an extra safety check.

Sway the gun on your wrist with your right hand only. Then, one-handed, lift the butt to your shoulder. The gun will feel top heavy. *Your right hand is your gun raising hand.*

Now lay your left hand round the forehand of the gun with your extended thumb pointing straight up the barrels in a line parallel with the extended index finger. *Your left hand is your aiming hand.*

With both hands in position, tuck the butt of the gun under your arm. It's no use holding the gun slackly with the butt at elbow-level. You must place the stock well under your armpit, and you must feel the wood with a squeeze between bicep and ribs. Generally speaking, it is a good notion to cant the barrels slightly skywards.

This is the first, or "ready," position for shooting.

(2) GO INTO THE READY POSITION. Right hand round the small of the stock, index finger extended; left hand round the forehand, thumb extended; the butt of the gun squeezed under your arm. In that position, use your left arm to push the barrels of the gun across your chest, so that they are pointing, not to the left, but straight in front of you.

At first this will seem an unnatural position. In fact, the position is the first step towards the achievement of consistent shooting. The stock is well-tucked under your arm so that, when you mount the gun to your shoulder, you give a forward push, and not a lift. A mere lift means that the barrels of your gun are swinging all over the place. A push forward means that your left hand, the aiming hand, is doing its proper job.

By thrusting your left hand into the arim, the recoil of the charge travels through your left arm, and down through your frame, which will take it like soft rubber. Otherwise, you would catch it on the shoulder where you find it hurts.

By squeezing the gun under your armpit—squeezing in the love sense—you are taking weight off your hands and helping the muscles in your arms to relax.

Most important of all, the ready position is a preparation for correct gun-mounting. It is a position designed to train you to thrust your shoulder into the stock when you fire. It will help you avoid the common error, the error which results in more misses than most, of dragging the stock into your shoulder.

Repeat: YOU MUST THRUST YOUR SHOULDER INTO THE BUTT OF THE GUN. THE GUN SHOULD NEVER BE MOUNTED AGAINST A FLINCHING SHOULDER.

There are other advantages in making the ready position a firm habit. It is the quickest form of gunmounting because the butt simply has to slip a few inches underarm to shoulder without losing contact (this is important) with your body. The gun comes smoothly, and naturally, without a snatch to eye level.

The gun comes up to your face instead of your head coming down to meet the stock. Faulty head movement, as I shall explain, is one of the commonest causes of faulty shooting.

The system checks hasty gunmounting, and encourages good timing. It will force you to start your body swing as the gun is coming to your shoulder. To adopt it comfortably, you will find yourself standing the way you ought to be, square on target.

(3) LOOK AT THE POSITION OF YOUR FEET.

Remember the trouble that good golfers take to find a balanced and comfortable stance. Good guns are equally particular. You will notice that, when game is driven over rough ground, experienced shots take care to secure a position for their feet in which they can pivot without obstruction. They stamp the ground in the way that a batsman taps the pitch between balls.

I appreciate that, in rough shooting, you may often be in a hide, waiting for wildfowl or pigeon, without being on your feet at all. Never mind. First, the drill is how to shoot standing upright on your two feet. The rest will follow.

With your gun in the ready position. look down at your legs. In the correct shooting attitude your body should be balanced evenly between them. If you are of medium height the toes of your feet should be about nine inches apart, and the heels about three inches apart. A taller man may extend his feet for comfort a little more. But it is better to take too narrow a stance than one which is too wide.

If you put a gun into the hands of a novice—an ideal subject for the experiment is the average girl—you will notice that, when she mounts it, she instinctively draws back her right shoulder from the butt, and advances the left foot. What is meant to be an aggressive stance is just the opposite.*

Don't splay your feet. You will be off-balance when you fire. The recoil of the charge will lift the butt from your shoulder to your arm muscles. You will probably bruise yourself, and you will assuredly shoot underneath the target crossing on the right, and over the top of one moving to the left. And you will be all over the place with the second barrel.

If you stand with your heels too close together you will find that you are taking recoil on your shoulder, instead of down your legs where you won't feet it. If

* See plate between pages 26-27.

you come home from a day's shooting with a bruised
cheek or a bruised second finger, don't blame the gun.
The chances are that you have been shooting from a
stance which is too narrow for you.

It is equally a fault to spread your legs too wide. Try
it, and you will find that you are unable to transfer your
body weight from one foot to the other without swaying
your trunk. The consequence is that, when you fire, you
will drop your shoulder and miss underneath. On rough
ground, recoil can knock you off your feet.

The ideal position is exactly the same position that a
good golfer adopts to swing a club. The balance on both
legs is even. Your body is poised to drain gun recoil
pleasurably through your boots. Without a gun in your
hand, it is the position in which you can swing your
shoulders rhythmically with only a minimal change of
weight from one leg to another.

When you are satisfied that you have found the
stance, pick up your gun in the ready position. Without
lifting your gun to your shoulder, practice a swing of 45
degrees to the right and to the left. The swing to the left
will transfer the weight on to your left leg. The swing to
the right will transfer it to your right leg.

Now increase the swing to 90 degrees in both
directions. You will find that, as you pass 45 degrees,
you raise a heel and pivot on your toes with
the movement. Ideally your stance should not change in a
halfcircle to left or right. In practice, especially on rough
ground, it is sometimes advisable to move one foot to
the rear of the other. But the theory remains.

ONLY ONE LEG MOVES. THE OTHER IS THE
PROP ON WHICH YOUR GUN IS MOUNTED.

At this stage of dry practice, resist if you can the
inclination to mount the gun to your shoulder. Keep the
butt tucked underneath your arm. The reason is that
more than half the misses in shooting are made before

gunmounting. You must get footwork and body swing right first.

It is so important that shooting coaches often demonstrate how, with correct timing and footwork, you will shoot straight at a moving target even if you press the trigger before your shoulder has bedded into the butt of the gun. Some snipe shots, although I don't recommend it, do just that in the field.

A lot of your shooting may be from a walking position. But don't get the impression that what I am telling you about footwork may be all very well for a man with a comfortable stand at a pheasant shoot, but not for a chap who has to march out and find his game. If you want to shoot straight, there's no difference.

However unexpected the shot, there is always time, if you cultivate muscle memory, to find your feet as you shoot. Remember that, if you let off with your left foot forward, you will shoot under the mark. If you shoot with feet together, you will be off-balance, and catch recoil. Your second barrel will simply be a waste of a cartridge.

There's always time—not to take aim with a shotgun, if you do that you will miss—to compose your body with your eye on the ball.

THE IMPORTANCE OF GRIP: I have explained how you can miss with legs. Later, I shall tell you how you can miss through faulty head movement. This lesson is to show you how easily you can miss with your hands.

Up till now I have counselled you, in dry practice, not to mount the gun to your shoulder. The secret of all arms drill, as any sergeant-major knows, is to· learn stage by stage, and to repeat it until the recruit hardly has to think what he is doing. And I can only insist that, if you want to be a consistently sound shot, you can't afford to dodge "the square bashing."

From the ready position, let's make an experiment.

Later on I shall have more to say about gun-mounting. For the moment, concentrate on hands. Most people believe that they grip a gun naturally and correctly. Check your own grip.

A common fault is to wrap the *right hand* too far over the top of the stock. Wrap your fingers as far round the small of the stock as they will go, and you will find that you can't lift the gun without raising your elbow as well. If you shoot from that position, the recoil will bash the knuckle of your second finger against the rear of the trigger-guard. Another fault is for shooters with a short thumb to keep it in contact with the top lever.

The correct position for the right hand is the one in which the small of the stock is sunk comfortably into the hollow of your palm. In that position, the ball of your trigger finger—the pad of your finger, not the first joint—should be lying along the guard just within pressing distance of the forward trigger. You should see a clear gap of daylight between the back of the trigger guard and the knuckle of your second finger.

When you fire, your right hand simply has the duty of lifting the stock from the ready position under your bicep, the mere six inches it should travel, into the thrust of your shoulder. Your trigger finger should scarcely move, because *triggers on shotguns should never be pulled.* All your trigger finger will apply is a slight stiffening in pressure to meet the thrust of your shoulder into the gun, the forward balanced movement of your whole body into the butt.

Your *left hand* is the ranging hand. Your left has to share the duty of lifting the gun to your shoulder; but your left hand is also *the aiming hand.* While it is self-evident that if you kill with a shotgun the muzzles must have been pointing correctly at the target, it is positively misleading to think of shotgun work in terms of barrel aiming; that is, unless your ambition rises no higher than sitting targets.

Repeat: THE BARRELS OF A SHOTGUN SHOULD NEITHER BE SEEN NOR HEARD.

All you have to make sure of is that the extended thumb of your left hand, lying along the barrel, is pointing in the right direction. Leave the gun to look after itself. *It will shoot wherever your left hand puts it.*

I can believe that, at this stage, you may find it difficult to accept the rule that good shots don't point with shotgun barrels. The "natural" thing to do—how often the natural theory is wrong—is to put the gun to your shoulder, aim up the rib, and pull. Shooting that way, it will be a fluke if you can puncture the hat of your worst enemy when he throws it in the air.

The system of shotgun shooting is that, if the left hand is moving smoothly on the mark as the gun is mounting, the barrels will be on the mark, too. We will come back to that, again and again, later. The secret of drill is repetition.

At this stage, pick up your gun by the small of the stock in your right hand. Make sure that it is comfortably cupped in your palm, that your trigger finger is extended within pad reach of the front trigger, and that you can see daylight behind the guard. Onehanded—it will help you to tone the right muscles—put the gun to your shoulder. You will find that it is barrel-heavy.

Now close your left hand over the forehand, with your thumb extended along the right barrel (not wrapped round the top of it). The correct position is when the distribution of weight is evenly balanced between your hands.

If the left hand is too far back the stock will mount earlier than the barrels. You will also feel recoil. If the left hand is too far forward the barrels will come up before the stock. Either way, you will miss. Find the point of balance where the gun comes up horizontally so that, by the time your shoulder thrusts into the butt, the barrels are more or less parallel to the line of your eyes.

If you have not used a gun much, practice of this sort will tire you. It is surprising how heavy, with excercise, six or seven pounds can be. To shoot straight, you must toughen yourself to it.

Now go back to the ready position. You may well have it right, but how tight are you holding your gun? My guess is that by this time, you are hanging on to it like a tug-of-war rope. Relax! In dry practice, get into the habit of hugging the butt of your gun under your arm as affectionately as a pretty girl, but as gently as one you cherish. It's only as you lift the gun to meet your shoulder that you should put on the pressure, tightening *only* at the moment that you touch the trigger.

If you try too much as you lift into action, you will relax as you fire, and miss. The movement, in ballroom dancing terms, is slow-quick-quick. In lovemaking terms—and, after all, a gun is a masculine extension—start gentle, finish hard.

HOW NOT TO BE OFF WITH YOUR HEAD: Robert Churchill used to say that head movement is the cause of one-half of the misses in shotgun shooting. You can prove it for yourself. Point your finger at any object. If you close one eye, you will find that you come on it at first aim every time. Now, lower your head as you raise your finger. Just notice how wide you are of the mark.

For shooting, you need to have a stiff neck. For guidance, practice with a gun in front of a looking glass. If you see your head coming down to meet the stock, practice until you are confident that you are not bending your neck to your gun. Shooting is a proud business in which a proud head is vital to success.

Your head should only move on your shoulders, with a gun in your hand, with the movement of your whole

MORE OR LESS RIGHT: Theoretically, this is the safest way to carry a shotgun. The gun is laid across the shoulder, guard uppermost, with a protecting forefinger over the triggers. The position is only dangerous if the barrels are permitted to trail. Not to be recommended because other guns don't know whether you are loaded or not; or what will happen if you chance to slip, or drop your barrels behind.

RIGHT: In practice, the safest way to carry a gun is broken under your arm. The gun carries better. Your friends can see that the chambers are empty. You will gain points for care; far more than you will for a killing shot, when others are unready. Make a rule that you will only get into the ready loaded position when the game is on. And you are in position to shoot.

T H E   I N S T A N T   O F TRIGGER-PRESSING: For a bird on the right, (1) the body is propped on the right leg. The left heel lifts and the left toe swivels in co-ordination with the movement of arms and shoulders on to the line of the target. For a bird on the left (2) the weight is placed firmly on the left leg. Shooting at ground game coming from the left (3) the weight is on the left leg and the shoulders lean forward to decline the body angle. At ground game coming from the right (4) the body sways forward on to the right leg. The pivot of the toe (5) and the twist of the heel away from the target enables the shooter to cover a field of 90 degrees on each side and to return, on the completion of the movement, to ready position.

BODY MOVEMENT AIMS THE GUN:
The positions frozen in the photographs
are, in actual practice, part of a
continuous stream of action. If the
movement is unbalanced, or if there is
the slightest hesitation in
trigger-pressing as the shoulder thrusts
into the butt of the gun, it will be a
miss. The reason (*see diagram*) is that,
although the shooter's eyes are on the
target at the instant of firing, the angle
of the barrels of the gun is in front of
the target. Thus, if the head is held
correctly, the necessary forward
allowance for a moving target is
automatically provided for. Any
attempt to line up the barrels on the
quarry, or to intercept the movement
by aiming at the air space in front, is a
fault. Glue your eyes on the target.
Your barrels, when you fire, should
never be in view.

**THE THEORY OF
AUTOMATIC
ALLOWANCE:** The
shooter's eye sees the
bird but the angle of the
barrels of the gun is in
front of the target at the
moment when bird and
barrels come into view
together. Thus, if the
head is held correctly,
the necessary forward
allowance for a moving
target is automatically
provided for.

THE READY POSITION: The gun is squeezed, but not squashed, between biceps and ribs. The pressure under the armpit should be just enough to relieve the weight. The gun is pushed forward across the chest. The trigger finger lies straight over the guard. An upward cant of the barrels helps.

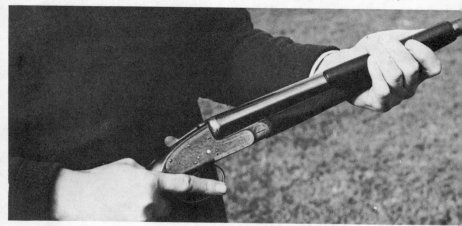

THE HALF-READY POSITION: It is easier to hold a gun, in preparation for shooting, at the stretch of the right arm. You are then ready to slip the stock under your bicep for the critical movement of correct gun-mounting. The essence of gunhandling is to use your weapon as an extension of your own limbs.

body. Don't hang it to kiss your gun. Raise the gun to your shoulder at the level of your head.

After all that drill, the secret that I want to impress on you is that you must master yourself. All you really have to do is to concentrate, keep your eye on the target, count it dead before you press the trigger, trust your first aim (you'll be in the soup if you look for a second one) and cultivate what I can only call an attitude of bloody-mindedness.

Nobody ever shot straight who was over-anxious. The bird that flies away is always the one you have promised the kitchen for dinner, or the one you wanted to show the chap with you you couldn't miss. Good shooting is seldom hasty, rarely over-cautious. You must master the drill; without it, you won't know why you miss a haystack, or hit it. But, with a sound knowledge of the elements of the game, you will always know *why* you miss.

The next chapter concerns what is probably the most critical process of shot gun shooting, for it coordinates all the mechanical functions of stance, footwork, head position and grip with the conscious function of aim.

6

Gun Mounting and Swing

If you point a finger at any object, you aim at it; unconsciously you adjust your line of vision behind the line of your arm. You don't have to make sure that you have sighted your finger correctly. You assume that the aim is true. And it is.

The art of gun-mounting is to lift your gun on to the target as naturally as you point your own finger. There is no need to check whether the aim is true. If you carry out the movement, *smoothly and unhesitatingly* the way you point with your own finger, you will be on target.

You will miss only if you make an unnatural correction thus disrupting the harmony of what you are doing. You cannot hope to point straight with your finger, for example, if your eye is looking in another direction. It is difficult enough to point straight if your body is off balance. It would be inconceivable if your arm was not joined to your shoulder. But one or another of those faults are the faults we all make when we miss with a gun. The drill is designed to eliminate them, to make a separate arm a part of yourself.

It seems simple enough on paper. In actual practice, the compound movement of gun-mounting calls for a conscious effort as complex as the unconscious effort of pointing a finger. You won't achieve it without a deliberate acquisition of muscle memory.

To begin, let's start at the climax of the lift because you won't get there if you don't know at the beginning where the butt of the gun needs to be seated in your shoulder.

The best way of finding the precise position is to fold your arms across your chest. You will notice that your shoulders round forward with the movement in just the manner that your right shoulder should come forward to meet the butt. With your left hand feel 'the slot' which the folded arms position has created between your collar bone and the ball in your shoulder socket. That is exactly where the butt plate of the gun should settle when you mount. Feeling it, you can almost believe that the human body has been anatomically fitted to take it.

Pick up your gun in the ready position, squeezing the stock under the gentle pressure of your bicep, and pushing the barrels away from your chest so that they are pointing not across your body but in front of you.

Now give the gun a slightly *forward thrust* with your left hand just sufficient to enable you to slide the butt plate up your arm to "the slot" in your advancing shoulder (the cross-armed shoulder position). The movement of the gun should be limited to the bare minimum to travel it approximately 6 inches from point to point. Ideally, the butt should never lose touch with the cloth of your jacket. The slightest clearance between butt plate and shoulder is all that is necessary, or desirable. The thrust of the left arm automatically provides it.

Look out that you don't make a meal of the job, see-sawing the butt and barrels. The action must be as economical in traverse as you can make it, the gun rising in even balance to the level of your eyeline. Remember that it is fatal to drop your head to meet the lifting gun.

Practice with a stiff neck until you find the gun

slipping smoothly into "the slot" in your shoulder, and the line of your vision.

This is the first lesson, but only the first lesson, in gun-mounting. It is simply an exercise in preparation for the critical business of trigger-pulling. In actual shooting practice, the butt of the gun will not meet the thrust of your shoulder except at the instant you fire.

So easy to tell, so evasive in the conditions of the field. But practice...practice...practice...will help you to command the situation.

Your instinct, especially when you are shooting badly, will mislead you again and again into putting the butt of your gun into your shoulder, taking a peep, and pulling later. You will be yards behind a moving target. You must discipline yourself to shoot on *first aim.* Second thoughts in game shooting are a sixpenny cartridge wasted.

The worst mistake you can make is to try and cut off a moving target by shooting at a bit of space in front of it. Leading your bird is as hopeless a system of shooting as trying to pick up an object with your pointing finer when your eyes are looking in another direction. You will make a fluky kill once in a while. What you will never make is a consistent shot.

I have explained the theory of allowance, because so few people seem to understand it, in a later chapter. But its interest, for practical shooting purposes, is eclectic. For the present, forget it. The knowledge of why you can shoot with a shotgun, *without conscious aim,* will not help you in the field to kill one bird more, or less.

Get the drill right; but remember that the drill is merely the exercise for field conditions. Even if you have learned to accomplish all the parade ground orders, your gun will be a lifeless log until you master AGGRESSION AND TIMING.

The top practitioners in all games recognize the

importance of the will to win. It is tremendously important in the sport of shooting. If you are shy of your gun, a little lacking in confidence as to your capacity to use it, or to shoot hard and straight at what you are aiming at, you might just as well be playing darts. The principle that if you grasp the nettle it won't sting is the principle of handling a shotgun.

A 12-bore can sting. It can knock a tooth out, bruise a lip or cheek, or bowl you over on your bottom if you recoil from it. But if you put your right shoulder into the work, cultivate a balanced action, and underline your determination with a swear word when you miss, you are more than half-way to the sound shot I want to make you. A sense of *controlled aggressiveness* is a vital attitude.

Timing means the smooth and balanced rate of lift of the gun from the ready position to the instant of firing. In practice, you will complete your gun-mounting quicker for a fast bird than a slow one. But ignore the reason why. Just trust your eye. Whether you hit or miss, providing the target is in range, will be decided during the brief lift of the gun from under your arm to your shoulder.

Waiting for a shot in the field, you should be holding your gun in the ready position firmly but without any sense of muscular strain. When you see the chance of a shot, glue your eyes on the target. Sway on to the correct foot and, at the same time, start a slow lift of the gun, increasing the pace as your eyes instruct you to follow. As your shoulder thrusts into the butt plate, harden your neck muscles, and stiffen your trigger finger—it is a pressure not a pull—to fire.

Y O U   M O U N T   Y O U R   G U N SLOW-SLOW-QUICKER-BANG AS YOU WOULD YOUR OWN ARM.

Most of this instruction so far is for the oncoming or

going-away bird in which very little body-movement is called for. If body-balance is composed, if the eye doesn't wander off the target, and if gun-mounting and trigger-pressing is well-timed and aggressively controlled, these are the easiest shots to take. But most shooting calls for a swing to left or right, or behind. This is where footwork is vital. Besides correlating gun-mounting and eyes, your whole body must pivot with the gun.

THE THRUST OF YOUR SHOULDER INTO THE BUTT MUST BE TIMED TO COINCIDE EXACTLY WITH THE COMPLETION OF THE BODY SWING.

Since most shotguns have two barrels, you may wonder why I haven't referred more to the second one. To begin with, concentrate on the successful use of the first. It saves money. I remember that Robert Churchill used to tell me that, at the start of a day's shooting, he was content to fire one barrel at the first six oncoming birds until he had run himself in. I reminded him wryly that, in the sort of shooting I was used to, I counted myself lucky if I got six chances all day. But, of course, the great shooting coach was basically right. Don't try and punch with two fists until you have made sure that you can deliver a knockout with one.

But, once you have mastered the rhythm of shotgun work, don't hesitate to use the second barrel; and use it quick. It is especially useful on occasions when, after trying too hard with the first, you have missed behind. You will discover how often you can make a clean kill with a slightly exasperated snap shot with the second. It is proof of the importance of first aim. But make a rule never to fire the second barrel, however quickly you do it, without dropping the gun from your shoulder, and mounting and swinging again.

There are born shots who can achieve balanced shooting with two barrels from one mounting. They are very rare. Most people are off target after recoil. Simply start again. You will soon learn how quickly you can recover your poise; much quicker, in fact, than any bird flies.

If it were as easy to acquire in practice what I have explained in theory, this manual could end here. But if it were easy, there would be no fun in shotgun shooting. Surprisingly, many of the born shots who hardly ever miss have difficulty in explaining how easily they hit. This is not much help for the rest of us puzzling to find out why we are so often off-target.

IF YOU KNOW WHY AND WHERE YOU MISS, YOU ARE MORE THAN HALF-WAY TOWARDS BECOMING A GOOD SHOT.

7

Learning Why You Miss

The value of DRILL and the importance of TIMING can be demonstrated in a way which, at first, seems like a conjuring trick. Watching another man's performance in the field, *taking care not to look at what he is shooting at but his style,* it is possible to assess with a high degree of accuracy whether he has made a hit or a miss. With experience, you will be able to achieve it yourself.

If you see a man windmilling his gun, dropping his head, pulling his shoulder away, fumbling with his feet, or hesitating for a poke at the target before snatching at the trigger, you may depend upon it that he has missed. But if you see the gun lifting calm-slow-quicker-quicker in a rhythmic thrust with the whole body leaning on the movement, you haven't got to look when you hear the bang to mark a clean kill.

These days, when so many people have home movies, and everybody knows somebody who has a miniature film camera, it is valuable to get a friend to make action sequences of your own performance. You will be able to spot your own faults.

In ball games, everybody recognizes the classic stroker player, the man with the controlled mastery of movement in every nerve and sinew. In the sport of shooting, too, you must play to the line of the ball, fix

62

your eyes on its movement through the air, make your stroke with unfaltering decision, and follow through with your gun. In fact, a man who can shoot two out of a covey of partridges in front, change guns with his loader, and kill another brace behind, achieves a balance of timing and movement comparable to a century in first class cricket. Very few can attain to that sort of perfection in marksmanship. But, with practice, anyone who can read the number of a bus at twenty yards can school himself into becoming, if not a great shot, a sound and consistent one. When you do it right, to the onlooker it will seem easy; more than that, you yourself will feel on your day that it is. But not even the best are on their day all the time. I want to help you to shoot yourself back into form when everything seems to be going wrong.

On a busy day in the field, you will often get the rough signal that you are shooting incorrectly because you will find that you are hurting yourself with recoil. If your shooting style was perfect—and nobody's is perfect all the time—you should theoretically stand up to five hundred rounds with no inconvenience except a healthy muscular fatigue. In practice, even the most hardened shots show a falling off in the graph of their performance after a hundred and fifty rounds, or so.

The sense of occasion, in addition to the effort of concentration, affects shooters too. Some men, who shoot well when they are alone, find it difficult to get the best out of themselves in company, especially strange company. They are tense and they try too hard. The excitement of unexpectedly good sport leads to errors in style, errors which will show in trifling discomforts. I have never heard of anybody who completely avoided them. But you should know the causes, and the way to set about overcoming them.

BRUISED SECOND RIGHT FINGER: One of the

most common of shooting complaints. It is caused by the back of the trigger guard hitting the knuckle on recoil. This happens for one of three reasons: (1) You have held the gun too loosely at the instant of firing with the consequence that you have taken recoil on the middle knob of your finger. (2) You have failed, in gripping the small of the butt, to leave any space between your second finger knuckle and the back of the trigger guard. You may well find that your forefinger has been hooked too far round the tringer. (3) You have raised your right elbow too high, thus slackening your grip when it must be firm.

Remind yourself, even if the stock of your gun is short for you, that you must hold back your right hand so that you only touch the trigger with the pad of your forefinger. If you can't do this with comfort, you would be well-advised to lengthen the stock of your gun with a pad over the butt. Alternatively, chronic cases can have a rubber umbrella ring looped over the scroll of the guard at the point where it hurts.

Gunmakers can supply material sedatives to mitigate various local conditions. But the best way is to eliminate them by making sure you have got the drill right.

BRUISED CHEEK AND JAWBONE: This is an affliction which commonly affects tall long-necked men like the writer. Short square men seldom suffer from it. It is a difficult fault to beat, especially in a hard day's shooting. Causes may be; (1) that the stock is mounting a trifle too wide of the correct gunmounting position; (2) that the head is held too erect; (3) that the head is lowered at the moment of firing.

Theoretically, you should turn your head slightly away to avoid the trouble. Don't sandwich the flesh of your cheek like a piece of ham between jawbone and stock.

I myself have never altogether learned how to fire several hundred rounds without giving myself a slightly swollen jaw. I am content to be vulnerable. Providing you don't flinch, a sore jaw doesn't seriously affect shooting performance.

GUN HEADACHE: This trouble befalls people who hold their heads too loosely. The old remedy of checking the vibration by biting a rubber band between the teeth is often effective. But far better to learn to stiffen the neck muscles.

BRUISED MOUTH, BRUISED ARM, BRUISED SHOULDER, BRUISED CHEST: Novices, firing shotguns for the first time, commonly split a lip or raise a bruise in full technicolor on the shoulder. It can be therapeutically useful to remind them what they have got in their hands. The causes are loose grip, weak gun-mounting, flinching and fear of recoil. The cure is to learn the elements of the drill; or give up shooting.

It is wise to regard any symptom of discomfort from shooting as the consequence of an error in style. If you eliminate it without artificial aids, it must improve your performance.

Learning why you miss, never blame your cartridge. It is possible, although the odds are against it, that you will miss because you have a cartridge which "cartwheels"—that is, the shot spreads out of the gun with a hole in the center of the pattern—or it "balls," which means that instead of scattering the shot, the charge travels as a blob. But you may assume that the standard modern cartridge throws an unbelievably regular pattern which opens up, as it leaves a 12-bore game gun, to give you a come of shot—between it has depth as well as width—about the diameter of dinner plate at the average distance at which most game birds, and clay-pigeons, too, are killed. In brief, your cartridge, provides you with a reliable and generous margin for minor errors of gunmounting.*

But if you are shooting with a borrowed gun, or a gun

* More about cartridges and shot sizes on page 96 *et seq.*

which manifestly doesn't suit you—for example, too long in the stock or too short in the stock for your own length of arm—you may be entitled to blame the gun. You cannot hope to shoot your best with an ill-fitting shotgun any more than you can look your best in ill-fitting clothes. I can only tell you that you can do something, if your limbs are limber, to fit yourself to a weapon by modifying your grip. But it is no use pretending that you will shoot as well as you would with a gun which fits you.

You can also miss because you wear the wrong clothes. Wildfowlers, and I don't blame them, have a way of padding up to protect themselves against the wet and icy blast on their dawn patrols. But heavy clothes militate against clean smooth shooting. Generally speaking, a marshland fowler should use a gun shorter by a quarter to half an inch in the stock than he uses, say, for pigeon-shooting in the roots and stubbles. For inland shooting, the best clothes are the same old clothes you have worn for years. Many of the crack rifle shots at Bisley, for example, will wear their old raincoats in bright sunshine to preserve the regularity of familiar pressures.

Robert Churchill believed that all shooting clothes should be loose. His ideal was not the Norfolk jacket with gussets on the shoulder blades, but what is called a Raglan coat, with sleeves dipping like wings under the armpits.

He was emphatic, and how much I agree with him, that a man who is shooting should not be wearing braces. Apart from the fact that the buckle is usually in exactly the wrong place when you are mounting, braces are an article of attire which restrain free movement of the torso. For shooting, you need to feel that your shoulder blades and your waist can move as easily as if you were naked. The Carnaby-street type is a disadvantage.

So far, after emphasizing the importance of drill, I have given reasons *why you miss.* I want to explain to you *how you miss;* and show you a method by which, however thin your pocket, you can teach yourself to correct mistakes.

You need two friends to help you. If a clay-pigeon trap is out of your class, Webley's makes a target launcher which throws, with a blank cartridge, empty beer and vegetable cans with excellent effect. You can also play with a hand-thrower from a good high stand; or construct a catapult with strong square elastic. However you contrive it, the object is to show a moving target, any sort of target, against the sky. One friend is needed to spring the trap, the other to stand behind you as an observer.

Your observer's job is to watch the shot in the air. Don't be surprised if, when you make the proposition, your accomplice regards you as a raving lunatic. To shooting men who haven't tried, the notion that you can see a charge of shot in the air is as preposterous as believing in fairies. But, once the knack is acquired of knowing where to look and what to look for, it is within the capacity of anyone with reasonable eyesight. It is the trade secret of professional shooting coaches. They can *see* where you are shooting.

During the war, it was commonplace for people behind a howitzer to mark the trajectory of a shell lobbing through the air. The howitzer shell is a big object, but the initial velocity is not much higher than a shotgun charge. To play this game, you have to get rid of the factor of personal disbelief. The observer can do it; if he can persuade himself that he can.

Don't imagine that anybody can see a swarm of individual pellets. What an observer *will* see is a sort of aerial disturbance. In soft light conditions, it is even possible to mark it like an exploding balloon.

The man who is shooting cannot see it. The reason is that, although we describe our cartridges as smoke-less, they throw a tongue of both smoke and flame. If you are shooting on a still day, in a heavy stagnant atmosphere, you will see the smoke. If you are shooting at dusk, you will see the flame, spitting about two to three inches beyond the muzzle. The muzzle blast of flame, smoke and a disturbance of hot gases about as big as an orange, screens the vision of the man whose shoulder is thrust into the butt of the gun.

At this juncture, I can imagine a keen shooting man reflecting that it would surely be simpler to use a tracer cartridge than set up the three-pronged operation I am recommending. Simpler, yes. Tracers are readily available, at a price; and, if you kill a bird with the modern sort, it will still be edible. The snag about tracers, although they look fine spouting out of the gun, is that, at the critical moment, the man who is using them loses sight of the line of the tracer behind the screen of muzzle blast and the barrel lift which accompanies recoil. An onlooker may have seen the charge pass in front of the target. The man who is shooting, temporarily unsighted by muzzle blast, supposes that he has shot behind because the bird has gone on, and the tracer line has stayed put.

If tracers were the answer, they would be used much more widely than they are. As it is, although most shooting men are tempted to try them out at some time or another, and although they give rise to a good deal of hilarity on days in the field, they are expensive and misleading. Far better to learn to see shot in the air.

As you cannot do it for yourself, you need the observer to spot for you; and, incidentally, your own shooting will be improved by spotting, in turn, for him.

The observer should stand behind your right shoulder

with his eye level set about three inches above the gun muzzles. He must search a point in the air on the line of shot and forward of the gun. If he looks at you or the gun, he will not see anything.

To begin with, it is sometimes a help if the observer stands on something like a soapbox for better elevation. But, with practice, it isn't necessary. If either, or both of you are sceptical, you may find that it is a help to make a practical experiment.

Choose a safe level place in which you can fire from a kneeling position at a double spread of one of the larger newspapers. Start from a range of 15 yards, and increase it shot by shot to 40 yards. Your observer should be a foot or two behind your shoulder, staring at the target just over the line of the muzzles of the gun.

If you regret the apparent waste of cartridges, I promise you that what you learn from the experiment will save you many more in otherwise wasted shots in the field. From the shot-holes in the sheets of newspaper you can read how your gun is patterning at different ranges. You can accustom yourself to estimating ranges correctly; and how shot, like water out of the rose of a watering can, spreads for every yard that it leaves the gun.*

But the chief purpose of the test is to help your observer to train his eyes.

Unless he is a very quick learner, it is unlikely that he will see any sign of the turbulence in the air made by the shot charge for the first twenty-five rounds. At fifty, if he concentrates, he ought to be seeing things.

If he isn't, it may be that he is suffering from what Robert Churchill called "observer's jump." What that means is that his concentration is diverted by the bang of your gun when you fire. You won't notice it yourself (or I hope you won't: remember the drill) because yours is the finger on the trigger. In your case, you are in the

* The important matter of judging range is discussed on page 78, in the chapter on Know-How in the Field.

position of a man who can squeeze the mess out of a spot in his own body without any nervous reaction. But the observer is the man who had somebody else squeezing for him. Not knowing precisely when the pressure is coming, he jumps. It will help the timing of all parties if the observer signals the trapper to throw up a target by sounding a whistle.

So as a temporary measure, especially if the disturbance in the air is evasive, get your observer to plug his ears. In time, when the sound of gunshot becomes monotonous, he won't need ear-plugs. He will accept it like the background music of the radio.

As soon as your observer reports that, in static shooting, he believes that he can see the flicker of a shadow, the ghost of the shot charge showing high or low on sheets of newspaper; and satisfies himself as well that the shot holes are more or less where he expected to find them, get on to flying targets.

Under a brilliant blue cloudless sky, so rare in Britain, he may be defeated. Under heavy cloud, so common in Britain, he will find that he sees shot rather more clearly than he did in ground level shooting. If you both stick at it, he will surprise himself, and you, with what he sees.

Once your observer has learned to *see* shot—and you have learned how to see shot for him—straight shooting ceases to be guesswork. Soon, you will discover that there are flying targets—to begin with, the oncoming slow bird—you can bring down again and again. But don't delude yourself that this is good enough.

In the shooting schools, when a man has got his confidence and is getting a little above himself, the form is to ask the trap springer to "vary them." When you see clay pigeons coming from all directions, perhaps two or even four at a time, your shooting will soon be reduced to size. But it is tests like that which raise performances.

So when your observer is confident that he can see

shot, get your trapper to "vary them." You will discover a whole heap of new shooting problems.

The professional shooting coaches look for a consistency of error. The difficult case is the man who is all over the place, never shooting with the same error twice. The explanation is often psychological, call it nerves; but it is always accompanied by bad discipline in the drill. For the rest of us, misses—once you know where you miss—are explicable.

After shooting with an observer for some time, you will even be able to explain your misses yourself. At first, the observer will be the one who tells you where you missed. With experience you will find that you can tell him not to tell you until you have made your own assessment of what you did wrong. Once you know what you do wrong; you won't have to worry much about putting matters right on a day when you are off-form.

You will find yourself saying: "I was behind that one because I poked and I was trying too hard, or I was off-balance, and I nearly fell base over apex when I took that one, or I missed him on the right because he curled." To make up for it, you will have those wonderful moments when you know, as your gun lifts, that you can count the target "dead."

Every shooting man has a pattern of temperament which can be conquered only with personal coaching. When your observer says, "you missed that crossing bird to the left, or you were miles behind that tall one," I can only generalize what your problem is. But it cannot fail to help you to study some of the most common faults, and the causes.

YOU ARE MISSING BEHIND: You are taking a second aim. You are hanging on the trigger. You are endeavoring to meet the bird in the air by pointing at the air space in front of it. You are being thoughtful, instead of trusting your eyes and body movement to bring you unerringly, as they will, on to the target. *You must point with your body, not your gun.*

In trouble, make up your mind that you won't shoot at the target, but a particular part of it. It doesn't matter whether you choose beak, wing, leg or tail, providing you glue your eyes at what you are shooting at. The pattern of shot will cover the lot. The important thing is that your eyes never leave the target.

Time your gunmounting to shoot sooner than the moment when the shot looks easiest. Don't wait for it. Let fly, coming up behind, as soon as the target fills your eye. Good shots kill their birds ten yards sooner than average shots.

YOU ARE MISSING BIRDS ON YOUR LEFT OR YOUR RIGHT: A right-handed man normally finds it easier to take a crossing bird moving from right to left than it is for him to take a crossing bird moving from left to right. The reason is simply that the body movement in taking the right-to-left bird comes naturally. The swing in the reverse direction is more difficult.

The solution is not to try too hard on a right-to-left bird. If your body-movement is sound, it is as easy as an oncoming one. Increase your determination when you tackle a left-to-right bird. In fact, it will mean that your gun-swing is quicker. Don't think about it. Just grit your teeth, and have at him. Rely on your eyes to carry your gun through. The answer is that you have just got to force your gunmounting a fraction quicker.

YOU ARE MISSING OVER YOUR SHOULDER: It is almost certainly the consequence of bad footwork. Men who miss in front often pull off showy shots behind. They shoot straight because they don't wait to think about it. In desperation, thay make a clean swing, and kill. It is far better to shoot in front, well in front. But you can learn from the lucky kills behind. If you miss, study the drill on feet.

YOU ARE MISSING GROUND GAME: You are shooting too much from your own height. Your whole weight should be canted forward on your legs so that, when the butt of the gun touches your shoulder, you are aligned between the ears of your target.

YOU ARE MISSING IN FRONT: An uncommon error. It could be that the stock of your gun is far too short for you, so that the barrels are up before you complete mounting. You will be a rare bird if this is your consistent fault.

YOU ARE JUST MISSING TO LEFT OR RIGHT OF TARGET: It is probable that the cast in the stock of your gun is too much one way or the other off your eye level. It may be that you are canting the barrels as you lift them. Make sure that, when you mount, it is a level lift. If that is not the fault, your gun needs re-fitting.

YOU ARE MISSING BELOW: You are possibly mounting the butt before the barrels. The butt could be too short for you. It is also likely that a rearrangement of your grip will help. Try lengthening your hold—a handgrip you can slip on will be an advantage*—on the forehand. Best by far is to have your stock lengthened.

YOU ARE MISSING ABOVE: Rare, like shooting in front. It is more likely to happen shooting at birds on your left and right. You are off-balance, and you throw you gun high. You have not got your eye on the bird.

Whether you practice on clay pigeons or beer cans, and however efficient you become at it, there is still a world of difference between shooting "cold" and the performance you put up in the heat of actual field conditions. In the first place, an inanimate target is predictable; starting fast, slowing, hesitating and falling. Live game starts slow, increases speed, and is unpredictable in behavior. So, under field conditions, will you be.

*See Extras, page 120.

8

Know-How in the Field

The immediate aims in the field, after the indispensable preparation of dry practice and shooting at inanimate targets, are (1) the acquisition of constant (but relaxed) readiness; (2) the calculation of ranges; (3) the conquest of the nervous trait of trying too hard.

Whatever you are shooting at, from the heady excitement of driven pheasants to flighting wood-pigeons, you won't do credit to yourself, until you are *collected* within yourself, Knowing yourself, controlling your impulses, recognizing what you do wrong, is three parts of the know-how in the discipline of the field.

READINESS: A lack of readiness is, in shooting no vice. In ball games and in all sport, except perhaps fishing, eagerness is a virture. In shooting, over-eagerness is often objectionable, and it can easily become a dangerous habit. I remember shooting pheasants beside a famous cricketer who, every time a bird came in sight, slung his gun as if he were snatching a catch in the slips. He was safe enough; but he was stealing the shooting from the guns on both sides of him. The rule, however rough the shoot and whatever company you are in, is to offer the courtesy of the shot that's wide for you (unless previously agreed) to the man on either side.

Readiness doesn't mean that, in a party, you are the

one man with a loaded gun when everyone else's is empty. Recollect the case of the unfortunate fellow who was so keen that he put a cocked and loaded gun on to the back seat of his car. There is an essential difference between readiness and over-eargerness.

Never mind if you occasionally miss because your safety catch has been left on. Never mind that you missed a chance because you fumbled when you were reloading. Never be ashamed that your gun was empty when, between stands, somebody else pulled off a showy shot. There's always another bird; and, if you put safety first, another day. But, when the game is on, you can do a lot to improve your own performance.

At this juncture, I suppose I ought to tell you that your safety catch should never be pushed forward until the moment when your gun is mounting to your shoulder to shoot. That is the classic style. In practice, I can only say that I have known very few shots who have mastered the habit. Most of the shooting men I have come across take the greatest care to hold their guns in a safe position against the possibly of an accidental discharge; but prefer to keep their weapons cocked in readiness for the chance of a shot. Personally, I have never doubted that the extra movement required to release the safety catch is a deterrent to smooth gun-mounting.

If you constantly carry your arms at a safe angle, you needn't in my view concern yourself with the catch. Anyhow, it is an untrustworthy safety device. Better far take out the cartridges and carry your gun, broken and empty, when you are not expecting shooting. When you are in the ready position, it is reasonable to slip forward the catch. You protect your trigger guard, up to the instant of firing, with your extended trigger finger.

Use the catch; but don't make a fetish of it. You will find that you are less likely to be caught at an unready moment.

More shots are missed, not because safety catches are not taken off, but because so few shooting men take the trouble to give attention to quick reloading. In a hot corner, it is a useful accomplishment, well worth practicing.

First, make sure that you are opening your gun correctly. To release the top lever, your first finger should be knurled over the right lock plate. With your thumb on the lever, squeeze both the lock plates and release the stiffest lever you are likely to come across.

To open the breech, hold the stock under your arm with barrels canted slightly sideways. This gives extra body leverage to assist smooth and easy opening. Draw down the barrels with your left hand, while the stock is still gripped between your right side and right forearm. Don't try to do it with your right hand, which should now be leaving the lever to reach your pocket, your bag or your belt, for fresh cartridges (assuming, of course, that you are using a self-ejector gun).

If you are carrying out the operation successfully, your barrels will drop to an angle of approximately 45 degrees to the stock under your arm. The gun, turned slightly sideways, will eject the expended cartridges away to the right, rather than over your right shoulder.

Whether you have got your cartridges in a bag or in your pocket, give them *a good shake* before shooting. The weight of leadshot in the heads of the cartridges compared with their lighter bases, will encourage them to turn heads uppermost. The advantage is that, when your fingers close on them, it is long odds that they will have settled in the best position for quick handling. If you are using a belt, they will anyhow be "heads up." If you are using one of the bandolier tubes, make sure when you fill it that the bases of the cartridges decant first.

If you have only fired one shot, reloading a single

chamber of a double-barrelled gun is a quick process. Where you are likely to be found out is when you have fired both barrels. It is a fact that the majority of shooting men make a double job of it. If there's no hurry, it couldn't matter less. But, in game shooting, it is always wise to assume that the best chance of the day will show at the moment when you are least prepared.

Quick loading yields far better results than snatched shooting. I used to know a great shot in Norfolk who had polished reloading to such precision that, when he was shooting he carried a third cartridge by the neck of the brass between his first and second right fingers. He reckoned that, if he had two birds out of a covey of partridges in front, he had time to reload one barrel and, with one gun, shoot a third behind. He often achieved it.

While a perfection of movement and timing like that is beyond most of us, it is still worth striving for. The art of slipping cartridges, like oil, into the chambers of a gun is a requisite of cool and unhurried shooting.

Try this: When you break your gun, your hand should be traveling towards the unfired cartridges. If you have shaken them, they should come to your fingers easily, brass up. As you collect them, make a movement so that one cartridge is more prominent in your hand than the top one by about three-quarters of an inch; in other words, pick up the two cartridges in an over-and-under position. Insert the nose of the higher cartridge into the right barrel, but don't let go of it. Using it as an axis, twist your wrist so that the other cartridge turns over the left barrel. Then let them both go.

On paper, it may seem a laborious business. But, if you take the trouble to master the twist, you will gain a reputation for the speed in which you reload.

Don't allow speed to relax your safety precautions. There is always the risk that, once the cartridges are home you lift the barrels to the stock of the gun instead of the stock to the barrels. When you ejected the spent cartridges, remember, the stock of the gun was tucked under your arm. Keep it there. Close the gun with a pressure of your right hand, with a slight forward inclination of your body. Some men favor a lift with a forearm under the stock to close the gun. Take your choice.

YOU ARE RIGHT, WHATEVER YOUR PERSONAL STYLE, IF THE MUZZLES OF YOUR GUN REMAIN INCLINED, IN RELOADING, TOWARDS THE GROUND.

THE CALCULATION OF RANGES: You will more often let a chance pass, within easy range of your gun, than take a shot which is outside the potential of your weapon. This is not what is usually said in books about shooting. With the admirable object of preventing sportsmen from pricking without killing at long ranges, the emphasis is usually the other way.

You centainly need to be careful when you are wildfowling, and to watch yourself when you are shooting at hares. More about that later.

But, in most shotgun work, the common fault is to exaggerate distances. If a pigeon, pheasant or a partridge fills your eye, it is very unlikely indeed that the bird is out of range. The fact that you *think* it is too tall or too wide is quite likely why you take second aim, and miss.

At ground level, most of us have mental standards of distance. It may be the length of a cricket pitch, a small bore rifle range, or some other familiar unit of measurement. Against the sky, height is far more difficult to calculate. Pigeons that look as tall as the clouds are often within reasonable range. Again and again, shooting men congratulate each other on shots which, in truth, never extended the gun.

The effective range of a shotgun is somewhere between 40 and 60 yards. It may surprise you, but it's true, that most game is shot at a distance of about 12 yards. A kill at 30 yards is exceptional. I can prove it to you. The average oak or elm, which looks tall enough, is seldom taller than fifty to sixty *feet*; that is twenty yards or so. The average third floor window-sill is a mere twenty-four to thirty feet above ground level. So much for the birds that come higher than the trees.

It's a good policy in the field to practice your eye at gauging distances. If you are standing forty yards away from a belt of trees, for example, and the trees are ten yards high, the extreme distance when a bird tops the trees will be about forty-five yards. And you will be more likely to overestimate the range than otherwise.

To teach myself, I remember sharing a stand with a brilliant shot whom I challenged to shoot any bird that came over—it was a pheasant drive—quicker than I could. He beat me again and again. He was dropping birds ten yards earlier than I reckoned that they were within killing range. He was the sort of man who is welcome on any shoot. The sort of shot who is unwelcome is the one who blows good game to pieces at close range.

Robert Churchill was fond of saying that the time to shoot is when the bird "looks big enough to eat." It suited his way of timing the instant to shoot, but it may not suit you. In good light conditions, it is a fair rule for some people to say shoot when you see the white ring round a woodpigeon's neck, the eyes of an oncoming partridge, or the color of a pheasant. In bad light, if you wait for that, you won't shoot at all. Best of all, when you are looking for the chance of a shot, cultivate the habit of measuring instinctively the distance between yourself and a hedge, fence or straw stack. Get it into your head that a big tree is rarely more than twenty yards high. When you believe that you have pulled off a very long ground shot, pace out the actual distance. You will be surprised how easily an estimated forty yards turns out to be twenty, and less.

A pigeon hide is the ideal place to accustom yourself to reckoning distances. You are posted at a fixed point. You are likely to be shooting at all angles; and you have the opportunity of planting your decoys at paced ranges.

In inland shooting, the only animal of the chase which you are likely to think is nearer to you than she actually is is the hare. Because the hare is the largest quarry in the English fields—even a full grown hare in poor condition is twice the size of a rabbit—estimates of range can be painfully misleading. Theoretically, hares are usually so easy that a reasonable shot should never miss them. In fact, they are missed—and, worse than that, wounded—again and again through miscalculations of distance because of the hare's size.

A RULE, YOU WILL NEVER REGRET IT, IS TO HOLD YOUR FIRE AT A HARE UNTIL YOU SEE HER BIG EYES.

The shooting man most likely to shoot at wild ranges is the coastal wildfowler. Usually the most enthusiastic of shooting men, often the fellow with the thinnest pocket, shooting as he usually does in the deceptive half-light between daylight and darkness, he is the man who must constantly remind himself that, unlike inland game, *fowl are more often out of range than within it.* Fighting duck and geese are constantly pricked (1) because fowlers get trigger happy after a long wait, (2) because the absence of landmarks in typical wildfowling areas makes every object that appears seem nearer than it actually is, (3) because the variation in the size of fowl makes a goose crossing at one hundred yards look as big as a mallard at twenty yards; and a mallard at sixty yards as big as a teal at twenty yards.

A wildfowler shouldn't venture on the saltings at all, apart from the personal perils which that tough sport involves, until he can identify pretty well any fowl by silhouette and characteristic flight. The most successful wildfowlers are all first class naturalists.

HOW TO CONQUER THE FAULT OF TRYING TOO HARD: Notice, when you are shooting yourself or watching others in the field, how often the best shot of day is one in which a bird is pulled down which shows momentarily in a gap among the branches of the trees. It appears to be a demonstration of extra-readiness. It is nothing of the kind. What happens is that the gun, with no chance for second thoughts, has to fire on first aim. Doing that, he surprises himself with the speed that he is on target.

For contrast, compare the situation when the guns are standing back from a field of roots with the opportunity of watching birds travelling for perhaps a hundred yards before they are in range. They are missed again and again. The reason is that the guns are *over-ready*. Watching the birds coming, they take false aim, keep on changing their minds about the moment to shoot; and, in the end, shoot too late, and miss far behind what should be easy birds. It calls for a good deal of discipline to watch even a pigeon, never mind a pheasant or a covey of partridges, approaching from a distance.

A method which many experienced guns adopt, knowing how to time the speed of approach of birds, is to look at the ground until they estimate that the target should be overhead. Only then do they look up and shoot on first sight. This is true readiness.

But suppose you find that you are missing through over-anxiety—the vie of too much readiness—there are various wrinkles to correct the fault:
(1) Try to get your timing right—let's suppose it's a cock pheasant coming over—by saying quietly to yourself as your gun mounts: "WHAT-A-BEAUTIFUL-CHAP-YOU-ARE!" You fire as you spit the word "ARE."

(2) Hold your fire until the bird is almost over your head. Throwing your gun, leaning back with your left foot on its toes, your weight balanced firmly on the right, catch him just before you lose him from sight. The notion is to force you, from your body position, to shoot at first aim.

(3) It may help to affect a deliberate loss of temper. Tell the bird, with what ornamental four-letter language you like, what you think of him. It is often helpful to force that extra feeling of aggression which is the difference between killing cleanly in front and trailing far behind.

(4) Make up your mind that you will shoot the next bird that comes in the left or right wing, beak or tail—it doesn't matter what part of the anatomy you choose—and, when he comes, look at nothing else. If your eye doesn't wander, you will kill. The pattern of shot will cover the whole target.

(5) Notice that when you are in bad form—I hardly care to reccommend this, I simply state the fact—you will sometimes find that you shoot straighter, after you have drowned your sorrow in the middle day, than you did when you believed that you were on your toes in the morning. The reason is that you were missing in the morning through over-anxiety. Once you stop trying, the habit of good style asserts itself. I have sometimes noticed in my own case that, after regrettably sitting up all night playing cards, when I needed matchsticks to keep my eyes open in the morning, I have often shot far better than I did when I was in good nick the day before.

I repeat that the policy is not to be recommended, for obvious reasons, The moral is that, when you are shooting, you will shoot far better, once you have mastered the drill, with a readiness which is casual rather than forced.

Perhaps the best example of what happens to a shot

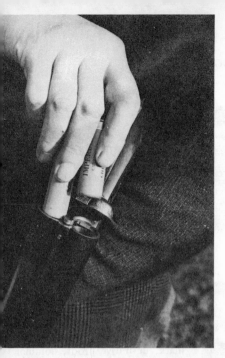

Top left: The over-and-under method of holding cartridges for quick reloading *(see page 76)*. *Top right:* The stand-at-ease position which must be adopted when charging a muzzle-loader *(see page 112) Bottom left and right:* Mounting and dismounting a gun should be carried out as a drill. When the forehand is taken off to bend the breech of the gun, note that the forehand is not put on one side, but grasped against the barrels above the loop *(see page 105)*.

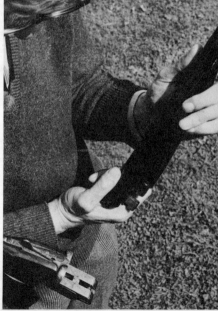

THE LONDON PROOF HOUSE

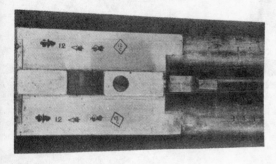

These marks show that the gun has been proved *for black powder only*. They are found on guns made as late as 1925; but if you see them it generally means proof before 1896. It is dangerous to shoot cartridges loaded with nitro powder through these barrels.

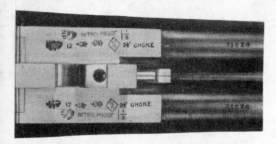

Guns carrying these London marks were proved between 1925 and 1955. From left to right, the marks read: Provisional proof, bore size, view mark, definitive proof, nominal bore size, chamber length, nitro proof mark, maximum charge of shot in ounces.

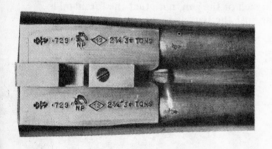

The London marks (under the 1954 rules) introduced on February 1, 1955. From left to right they read: Provisional proof, bore size, nitro proof, nominal bore size, chamber length, highest mean service pressure for which gun is proved.

Note that the proof marks on foreign arms are different. By reciprocal agreement with the English proof authorities, guns made in Belgium, France, Italy and Spain are accepted under their own national marks. Guns made elsewhere—notably in the U.S.A., where there is no official

THE BIRMINGHAM PROOF HOUSE

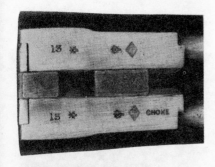

Marks which show that the gun is proved for black powder only, and is therefore unsafe under the additional pressure of modern nitro powders. Guns carrying these marks date to 1904, when the crowned mark changed, to the BV. BP. NP. type below.

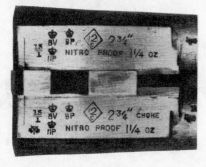

This is the most common type of marking found on used shotguns. It shows the nitro proof marks which became compulsory in 1925, and includes details of chamber length and shot load. This gun is safe for use with modern powders.

The series of marks introduced in February, 1955, which gives details of service pressure to the square inch. The mark at the bottom left corner—in this case LBI—is the private viewer's mark which in code gives the name of the viewer who passed the gun and the year in which it was proved.

proof—are re-proved on import in London or Birmingham. You can recognize them because the flats on the barrels are marked "NOT ENGLISH MAKE." Insular, yes; but, in the rules of gun safety, this country has led the world.

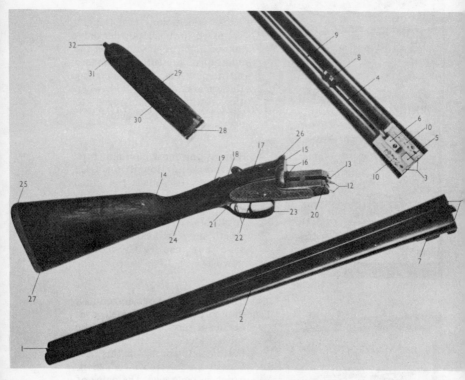

PARTS OF A GAME GUN: BARRELS: 1. Foresight. 2. Top Rib. 3. Extractors. 4. Keel Rib. 5. Rear Lump. 6. Forward Lump. 7. Hook. 8. Fore-end Loop. 9. Bottom Rib. 10. Flats Showing Proof Marks. 11. Chambers.

STOCK AND ACTION: 12. Cocking Levers. 13. Extractor Cam. 14. Comb. 15. Action Face. 16. Striker Holes. 17. Top Lever. 18. Top Strap or Tang. 19. Safety Slide. 20. Knuckle. 21. Lockplate. 22. Triggers. 23. Trigger Guard. 24. Chequering. 25. Heel. 26. Screws (called Pins by Gunmakers). 27. Toe.

FORE-END: 28. Ejector Kickers. 29. Chequering. 30. Fore-end Diamond. 31. Fore-end Tip. 32. Release Button.

trying too hard is what goes wrong when a covey of partridges explodes in front of him. Partridges, by comparison with wildfowl and pheasants, move at a mere 25 m.p.h. It is significant that single birds, often "Frenchmen," are almost always shot. In theory, coveys shouldn't be more difficult.

In practice, the appearance of a covey of partridges, with old birds leading as they always do, panics many shots. It seems that there are so many birds in the air that nothing is required except to let fly "into the brown." Guns are then surprised to find that the whole lot pass unscathed into the blue.

The explanation is that the shooting man has fired, not at an individual bird, but at *the air space in between birds.* Because first aim is always correct, he is making sure, unless he flukes, that he has missed the lot. The solution is to concentrate on one bird, however many birds are in the air. Pick a wing, a tail, or the beak, of a one bird only; and you will find that you are dead-on.

It is hopeless, when you see the chance coming of a right and left, to look for two birds at once; whether it's woodpigeons, wildfowl, pheasants, partridges, or grouse. It is essential to fix your eye on one bird, and shoot him as far out in front as you can. Unless you are in the most controlled form, lower the butt of your gun from your shoulder, after firing the first barrel, into a half-ready position, and pick the second bird on first aim again. You will have plenty of time to do it. Straight shooting is never flurried, however quickly the gun moves.

You may well put up a better performance if you condition yourself never to think, until after the event, of the achievement of a right and left. Concentrate on getting one bird; that's good enough by most shooting standards. Then balance yourself, not for the brace, but just to get another *one.*

THE RULE IS THAT, IF YOU ARE LOOKING FOR A

LEFT AND RIGHT, YOU WILL ALMOST INEVITABLY
SHOOT IN BETWEEN. FIX YOUR EYES ON ONE BIRD
AT A TIME.

In company in the field, you will inevitably watch other
people. During drinks afterwards you will be listening to
them.

In the first place, you may well find that you meet
dead-eyed Dicks who don't seem to do anything that I
have recommended to you in this manual. Next, if you ask
them how they get there without the drill, they will look
at you with blank faces. They just do it. A lot of
gamekeepers are like that. They use a gun as if it were a
third arm, untidily to the eye, but with an effective
cross-bat technique of their own. It often comes off among
men who are raised in green places. But I can't recommend
it.

Don't be deceived by men, who can shoot the tip off a
cigarette, who claim that you can either do it, or you can't.
You can do it, too. If you cultivate style, you can become
the sort of shot who looks classic, even when you miss.
And you won't miss nearly so often.

I recognize that a lot of your shooting won't be in
comfortable places when you have a stick to support your
behind. You may be in a hide looking for pigeons or
wildfowl. The drill is the same. What you have practiced
on your feet, you must learn to apply when you are lying
on your face, or on your back, whether you are crouched
in a hole in the ground, or down at the bottom of a creek.
You will miss if your gunmounting is at fault.

*What you must do is to learn to swing your gun with
your hands and shoulders alone.*

You won't do that unless you have mastered
gun-handling and gunmounting in the standing position. In
the crouched position, your body, from the waist upwards,
must move as if you were handling your gun in an upright

stance. You must come up behind your bird with the swing of the waist; and, on the round of your bottom, keeping the top-half of yourself, as free as you know, on target. It is not so difficult as it sounds in description.

If you miss, your head is probably at fault. It may be that your head is coming down to the gun, or going too far back. If you miss behind, your shoulders are not following the bird. It may be that, in a cramped position when your legs are immovable, you haven't allowed complete freedom of arm and chest movement; otherwise you could be wasting your effort.

In a hide, especially under trees or after pigeons, there will be times when you get the offer of a sitting shot. Hitherto, I have only discussed flying birds. If you want to knock off a sitter on a tree, the only time I recommend you to look at the bird over the end of the muzzles of your gun, *shoot at his legs.* If you shoot at his head, you will miss high.

In all sitting shots, the trick is to shoot lower than seems probable. Aim at the legs of a pigeon in a tree and, in ground shots, place the charge with the general objective of lifting the ground underneath what you are aiming at.

This rule applies to hares lolloping towards you in a drive. A going-away hare, starting from her form, should be dealt with differently. What you must aim to avoid is wounding her in the flanks. Fix your eyes between the V of her long ears at the point where you would place the foresight of a rifle in the backsight. Just fix your eyes, don't hang about over the head of the gun. Providing you shoot on first aim, you should bowl over your hare clean dead.

In the shooting field, you will hear all manner of claims about shooting performance. You can disbelieve most of them. I have seen a man shoot two partridges in front, change guns and shoot two behind, about three times in my life. I think—I am not sure—that I have seen a man with three dead pheasants in the air. Personally, I lay claim to the record that I had the chance of killing an easy right and left at woodcock, with a boottle of *Bols* gin as my reward; and, in my excitement, missed both of them *(I was trying too hard).*

In your case, discount any claim—it doesn't matter anyhow—of shooting proficiency. You will hear people say that they have killed 75 per cent of the pheasants they have shot at. What they don't tell you is how many cartridges they have wasted getting them.

In all shooting, rich man's and poor man's shooting, he is a first class shot who can show an average of 25 per cent kills to cartridges. Experienced shots can put up a better performance than that on inanimate targets. In the field, others will think that you are rather good if, when you wryly count up your expenditure of cartridges against your contribution to the bag, you have done as well as 20 per cent. At that percentage, you will have shot more than your share.

I recall a shot in which, after the day was over, we were all asked to write down on a scrap of paper what we estimated we had killed. The last man wouldn't join in. "When we learn the total bag" he said, "I'll bet I owe fifteen birds to the rest of you." He was the best shot among us; and sure enough, when the bag was declared, he was right.

People who boast about their shooting are seldom the best shots. Never talk about your own performance, however satisfied with yourself you may be; and don't count the birds you only think you hit. Other people don't miss much of the game.

9

Knowing What You Don't Do

I would prefer, because my sole object in this manual is to make you shoot straight, to leave this chapter out. But, unfortunately, you will meet shooting men, still far too many of them, who will try to suborn you with tales of how you should lead a bird thus or thus. You will meet the man who will tell you that, although he gave yards to a skein of wild geese, the one he killed was three behind the one he shot at. You will even hear that the way to pull down tall pheasants is to start shooting before you see them. A favourite form of advice is that you ought to have led that pigeon you missed by such-and-such a number of yards.

Let's begin by demolishing the theory of forward allowances, aim by calculation against aim by instinct. Ballisticians have worked out the figures.

The velocity of a standard 12-bore cartridge, over varying ranges, is known. As a simple example, 40 m.p.h. is the average speed of pheasant in full flight. From that, it can be computed that the gun muzzle movement necessary for forward allowance at a crossing bird, so that the pheasant and shot charge meet at the same time is:

1 1/2 inches at 20 yards
1 5/8 inches at 30 yards
1 3/4 inches at 40 yards

87

From this, one may calculate that, in general terms, a slow bird needs only half the allowance of the fast one and the birds at 20 yards only require 40 per cent of the allowance theoretically necessary for the 40 yard bird. Even these figures only relate to the bird crossing at right angles. For a bird quartering at 45 degrees all figures have to be halved. The bird seen straight in front, unless it is climbing steeply, needs even less allowance; and, if a bird twists as you lift your gun, no calculation of forward allowance is any good at all to you.

I could give you more tables. But it is enough to show that forward allowance for a bird crossing at 30 m.p.h. is approximately.

> 2½ feet at 20 yards
> 4 feet at 30 yards
> 6 feet at 40 yards

These figures, of course, are worked out on the basis of the time it takes for the charge to travel from the end of the gun muzzle. The man behind the gun should consider personal factors like the time it takes him to pull the trigger, and he should also make allowance for the lag in his weapon while lock mechanism and primer are igniting the charge. If birds flew at a level speed, if we had range-finders, and provided that we didn't lose a fraction of time in pulling the trigger after making the mathematical calculation, forward might work. As it is, I hope that I have said enough to prove that the judgment of forward allowance is beyond the capacity of the most expert shot.

Shooting men, who talk about the forward allowances they give, are talking verbal nonsense. All systems of shooting at moving targets founded on "allowances" are inherently unstable and unscientific. The good shots who talk that way don't practice what they preach; otherwise, they wouldn't be good shots. Bluntly, they simply don't know how to express in words what in fact they really do.

You need never concern yourself with forward allowance; indeed, you will certainly miss if you distract yourself by messing about the arbitrary predictions. Anyhow, you are wasting effort because *your eyes are the most beautiful calculating machine of all.* Fix your eyes on the target, regulate your gunmounting to suit the convenience of your sight, and the job of forward allowance will automatically, and exactly, be done for you.

What happens is this; shooting at a quickly moving target, your eyes move more quickly. Consequently, your body work is quicker. At a slow target, your gunmounting is more deliberate. In fact, if you are shooting straight, your eyes are working out all the complex mathematical problems of interception.

The diagram between pages 54-55 will help you to understand why this is so. Your eyes are on the bird, but the barrels of the gun are in fact in front of the target at the moment when your right shoulder thrusts into the butt. So if you don't hesitate with your trigger-pulling, and you don't drop your head, forward allowance for a moving target is automatically provided for.

It is true that the rate of lift in your gun-mounting, the confident trigger pull at the moment your shoulder thrusts into your gun, are essential concomitants to straight shooting. But the correct rate of lift is something you needn't even think about, subtle as the movement is, providing you fix your eyes unerringly on what you are shooting at.

YOUR EYES WILL TELL YOU INFALLIBLY WHEN TO MAKE THE SLOW-QUICK AND THE SLOW-QUICKEST LIFT OF THE GUN.

When you miss, ask yourself: (1) Was I off balance on my legs? (2) Did I hesitate, through lack of confidence in myself, before I pressed the trigger? (3) Did my eyes wander off the target? (4) Above all did I follow the advice of the damned fools who tell you to shoot at a patch of air in front?

10

Small Bore Rifles

This manual is mainly about shotgun shooting because Britain is primarily a shotgun country. The reason for it is that, outside the moorlands, the landscape largely consists of small hedged fields and small areas of woodland *in which you can't see what is on the other side.*

Although a shotgun needs using with unremitting care at ground levels, small shot exhausts its effective energy somewhere not far in excess of a 100 yards range. Anybody who shoots regularly in company will have experienced the patter of spent shot, fired quite safely by another gun, raining harmlessly on to him out of the sky. For contrast, here is a strange true story of what .22 rifle, innocently called a "miniature" rifle, can do.

Two boys were sitting on a fence watching a football match. Suddenly, one of them rolled off the fence, dead. The post mortem showed that a small bore rifle bullet had penetrated the back of the boy's skull, travelling in a downward direction. The police concluded that he had been shot by someone sitting in a nearby tree. There were no houses in the vicinity, and the boy's companion said that he was intently watching the game, which implied that his head was in a natural position. Murder was suspected until Robert Churchill was asked for his expert advice.

He examined the bullet, and made a mathematical calculation of its trajectory from the angle of the wound in the boy's head and the position he was sitting on the fence when he was shot. "I knew," Churchill told me afterwards, "that a .22 long rifle bullet could carry 1,200 yards, and I reckoned that this one might have been fired at a high elevation about a thousand yards away." It was the rook shooting season. Churchill asked the police to find out if there was a rookery at the distance he indicated, and in the direction in which he pointed. There was. It turned out that three Territorials had been shooting, with rifles borrowed from their regimental armory, at the time the boy was killed. Under the microscope, Churchill compared the bullet with the rifling in the barrels of the guns. He was even able to prove which of the three rifles had fired the fatal shot.

It is a fact that hundreds of thousands of rounds are let off at young rooks in high trees every season, usually without accident. People are encouraged to think that .22 rifles are the correct sporting weapons for the job (as indeed they are in lonely places) because they are often described as rook rifles. Nevertheless, I hope that the moral tale I have told you will be a lifelong reminder that *a .22 rifle can kill at a distance of one mile.*

It is important to appreciate that a .22 isn't just one sort of gun. The calibre represents a wide range of different types of weapons. You will find that you can buy a .22 rifle, designed to fire a calibre .22 cartridge (called a Hornet) with a very light bullet, high velocity and flat trajectory suitable for shooting vermin at 100-150 yard ranges. Alternatively, you can have a gun chambered for short cartridges, the sort of gun used in fun fairs to knock down ping-pong balls. The one you are most likely to be interested in is a rifle chambered to fire what is called a long-rifle ruin-fire ammunition.

If your interest is fixed target shooting, my advice to

you is to join one of the many small bore rifle clubs. In the club atmosphere, you will find people who will coach you in shooting straight at card targets. After shooting with club rifles for a while, you will be better able to make up your mind what sort of match rifle you want as your own because taste and eyesight, and gunsights, are widely variable. Anyhow, you should choose a match rifle, out of knowledge and with care, because the heavier guns, suited for high precision shooting, are generally more expensive than sporting arms.

But match-shooting, fun though it is, is outside the range of this book, which is concerned with field work.

As I have said earlier, it is rare for a man to be a first class performer with a match rifle on the ranges and with a shotgun at fast moving targets as well. The required attitudes are irreconcilable. The one, the man with the precision rifle, must control his breath and his body until he is as steady as stone. The other, the man with a shotgun, must swing and follow through like a golfer. If he stops to aim he has missed.

The sporting .22 shot uses a technique somewhere between the two. Indeed, it is possible, swinging a rifle like a shotgun, to shoot a single bullet as effectively as a pattern of shot. I have seen Afrikaner farmers, who learn to shoot almost as soon as they can shake a baby's rattle, bring down running buck with a rifle from the saddle of a moving horse. They even regard it as a not unusual achievement.

During his own career, Robert Churchill built half a dozen .22 double-barrelled rifles which were designed to bring down flighting wildfowl at long ranges. They were the fancy of a Long Island millionaire. I shot with them; and I was astonished how often, with a single .22 bullet, I split a flying clay.

The answer is that, if you are on your day, you would kill with a shotgun if only a single pellet came out of it.

Generally, that is no way to use a sporting rifle; but it is not unimportant to emphasize, once again, how accurate first aim can be.

Although the opportunities in my country are limited for the sort of shooting I am discussing, the miniature rifle has an important place for vermin control. As a vermin destructor. it is far more economic in what it costs to shoot than a scatter gun. Stalking your quarry, you will get the offer of shots—for instance, a grey squirrel frozen on the branch of a tree—in which you will have time to steady your sights and take careful aim. Mostly, you will bring up your rifle rather more slowly than if your were handling a shotgun. You will see your foresight, and the V or U of your backsight; but you mustn't make a meal of it.

If you hang on the sights, you will wobble. You yourself enjoy unusual vision if you can clearly see the backsight, the bead of the foresight, and the target, in proper perspective at the same time. Most of us don't. If you stop to take careful aim—at a crow on a fence, for instance—the bird isn't going to wait for you.

The secret, it's one that every gamekeeper knows, is to glance your sights, and, without hesitation, fire.

TRUST FIRST AIM.

You will be tempted to invest in peepsights and telescopic ones. My advice to you is that the best rifle to start with in the field is an open sighted arm. You don't even want one with a slide for different ranges on the backsight. If your weapon is ranged for fifty yards, you won't be far off the mark. Don't start your shooting career with artificial aids.

Have peep sights if you want to. They have the advantage that they can be hinged out of vision. But learn to rely on the set of the bead of the foresight, at six o'clock on the target, in the backsight. You can spoil yourself as a natural shot with gadgets. After all, you can always add them later.

The sort of small bore rifle to choose is essentially a matter of what you can afford. I have never been satisfied that an automatic confers any advantage in the field over a simple bolt action or, alternatively, what is called a trombone repeater. I don't think that it really matters whether the rifle is designed to load fifteen rounds, five, or one. Game isn't so thick on the ground that the speed in which you can reload is important.

You may depend upon it that any standard small bore rifle you buy—some of the best rifles, unlike shotguns, are made on the Continent—is a reliable weapon. I personally prefer to shoot with one with a broad grip in the forehand and plenty of wood up the barrel. I find that the sights settle more easily and quickly on the target.

But it is all a matter of personal fancy. It is really no advantage to have a gun you can shoot, as if you wanted to, like a machine gun; or one chambered to shoot with long and short ammunition. If the weapon has an efficient ejecting mechanism, to spare you breaking your fingernails removing empty cartridge cases, you won't in practice need more.

The short .22 ammunition, generally, is not to be recommended for shooting in the field. The solid long rifle bullet lacks stopping power. The hollow point bullet is the most suitable for vermin control.

Within the compass of this book, I must remind you again that shooting at still targets will probably be detrimental to your performance at moving ones. Much better, use your rifle, with a slightly more deliberate action, like your shotgun. It is good practice to get a friend to roll a target, such as a wind-fall apple or, if you are not that good, an ornamental gourd over level ground. Once you start hitting you will realize the importance, in the field, of not hanging on your sights. It will assist your confidence with a shotgun, too.

11

Cartridges

I can only suggest to you, half-hopefully, that you don't become a cartridge fanatic. But my expectation is that, sooner or later, you will join the theorists on correct shot sizes for different sorts of shooting, minimum and maximum loads, and even show a preference for cartridges with more brass or less brass in the base, or even of one color or another.

In the days of muzzle loaders *(see Chapter 13)* loads were a valid subject for gunroom debate. At the time, powder was variable, shot was often soft, or too hard, and badly-formed, and individual guns performed better with charges which had to be discovered by trial and error. I suppose that it is a sort of heritage from our forefathers that shooting men still like to think that the load is a matter for discussion.

It isn't. The modern standard cartridge is a good deal more reliable in performance than the modern mass-produced car. I have said elsewhere that you will get an occasional one which "cartwheels," or "balls," but, unless you see the evidence on a whitewashed plate, you can never be certain. It's always wise to remind yourself, whatever your private hunch, that it is still likely that it was your footwork, your gunmounting or the timing of your trigger pull that was really at fault.

Your cartridge is normally an obedient slave.

The difference between the cheapest standard cartridge you can buy and the best is mostly in the case. The most expensive ones are metal lined with deep brass bases to render them relatively waterproof. They look good in a gunbag; but, like the woman who wears Balenciaga on top, they are all very good underneath.

It may be desirable, in this egalitarian age, that paper cartridges of all kinds be dispensed with. Plastic cased ammunition—you can see powder, and shot charge inside them—have already been introduced by the Scandinavians; and latterly, the Americans. The F.N. Company in Belgium has been manufacturing short aluminium cased cartridges, with crimped closures, since before the war. But nobody shot a bird more, or less, because of them.

The cheapest paper cases can be a disadvantage to the wildfowler because, in soaking conditions, they swell. It can be a nuisance pushing them into the chambers of the gun and a worse nuisance hooking them out when the ejector springs are not strong enough to throw them clear. For that reason, every shooting man, if only to help his friends out of trouble, ought to carry a small cartridge case extractor (you can buy one for a few shillings) on a key ring.

If you find that you have swollen cartridges which stick in the gun you can re-size them with a re-sizer which you can also buy for a few shillings. But damaged cartridges are best employed at targets which you don't mind missing.

There are connoisseurs who can identify different brands of whisky. There are shooting experts who can recognize, from the sound of the report and the recoil, one powder from another. Even the ordinary shot can quickly learn to distinguish between the straight slow push of black powder and the quick kick of the smokeless ones. Churchill could judge by ear the quick cartridge from the slow. I myself—almost anyone can acquire it—can tell whether a shot has been fired at flying game or ground game; whether it was a short-barrelled gun, with its sharp crack, or a long-barrelled one.

All these matters are part of the interest of going shooting, the interest which, if it's enthusiastic enough, encourages straight shooting. But the theoretical fun must be kept in perspective. Whether you shoot straight depends on you, not the noise out of the gun or the spit out of the cartridge.

Even if you accept that powder and shot is now so reliable that, for all practical purposes, you can forget them, you may persist in the notion that shot sizes count, They do, just a little bit.

Shot sizes can range from dust shot, which people used to use to wipe out clouds of sparrows, to single moulded bullets designed to shoot large game through cylinder barrels. The standard shot sizes *for inland shooting* today are Nos. 4 to 7. The difference between them is that a normal 12-bore cartridge, loaded with 1 1/8 ozs of No. 4's carries approximately 191 pellets; No. 5's 248 pellets; No. 6's 306 pellets; and No. 7's 383.* Obviously the heavier shot has greater energy at a given range than the smaller size; but the smaller size, with its greater number of pellets, has a closer spray of shot.

It is generally recommended that No. 4's are the most suitable for inland wildfowl and hares; Nos. 5 to 6's for pheasants and pigeons; and No. 7's, or even No. 8's, for snipe. The trouble is that the game won't cooperate. When you are looking for a snipe with a No. 7, the dog flushes a pheasant. When you are waiting for a hare with a No. 4, a flighting pigeon appears. You are surprised when you bring down the pheasant with the No. 7, and vice versa.

---

* Tables of shot charges and mean patterns are appended at the end of the book.

Further, in inland shooting, it is very seldom indeed
that the killing range of the cartridge is extended to its
limit. At average ranges a No. 7 is as lethal as a No. 4.
Once again, I must exclude hares which because of their
size constantly confuse shooting men into thinking that
they are nearer than they are.

*The moral is that, if you stick to No. 6's for all inland
game from the season's beginning to the end, you'll do
just as well as the man whose head is full of shot sizes.*

If you are on a marsh, where the quarry is exclusively
snipe, by all means use No. 7's, or even No. 8's. If you
attend one of those February drives to reduce the
number of hares, it is more humane to shoot with No.
4's. But you will almost certainly do just as well if, by
mistake, you take No. 6's.

I have emphasized that all my comments so far
concern inland shooting. They might well apply to
coastal shooting, too, providing that all wildfowlers made
sure that they didn't shoot until the quarry was in
reasonable range. Unhappily, because the chance of a
shot is often so infrequent, the temptation to shoot at
extreme ranges can prove irresistible.

In the past, wildfowlers "stretched" their range by
carrying formidable cannon like four-bores and eights. As
I have explained, the time it took them to heave them
on to their shoulders, and recover from the recoil,
cancelled any advantage they had in fire power. The gun
for the modern wildfowler is undoubtedly a fully choked
twelve-bore chambered for 3-inch cartridges. The best
shot sizes are No. 4's; and, if wild goose chasing is the
object of the exercise, No. 3's.

Magnum guns chambered for 3-inch cartridges will
take 2 3/4-inch cartridges as well. The 2 3/4-inch have
only fractionally less energy, and in the heavier gun
(preferably with a rubber butt pad) recoil is noticeably
less; but I cannot recommend them. The trouble is that

2¾-inch cartridges fit comfortably into the chambers of a light game gun proofed on for 2½-inch. It is easy to mix them up with the standard sort.

I write from bitter experience. One day on a hare drive, I was surprised that I was feeling so much recoil. I thought that it was my gunmounting at fault. When I got home, with a sore jaw, I found that the rib of my gun had been lifted almost clean off the barrels. When I sounded the barrels by swinging them gently on the loop against the side of a table they gave, not the bell-like note they should, but a dull thud. I checked my belt. They were No. 4's all right but I had picked up one filled with 2¾-inch cartridges.

Fortunately, it was a good gun, and the repairs it needed were minor. But it was an ugly lesson. Why it happened was because I had 3-inch, 2¾-inch, and 2½-inch cartridges all of the same make and color. I have taken care that it can't happen again.

Although I made a ribald comment at the beginning of this chapter on men who believe that they shoot straighter with hand-loaded cartridges with fancy cases of one color or another, it is a precaution, especially if you collect an arsenal of weapons, to separate cartridges for different purposes by color or by the name of the gunmaker who loaded them. The shotsize is, of course, marked on the top end.

If you become one of those enthusiasts who load their own cartridges you can test your own efficiency at the job by taking a sample cartridge and, rapping the brass base, apply the pressure of your finger to the top ward. If it moves under the turnover, it means that you haven't packed strong enough. But it will be a very bad cartridge indeed, and a rare one, which doesn't kill at 20 yards.

Although I confess that I have experimented more than most, and although I wouldn't dissuade you from learning about cartridges by filling them yourself, in my heart I know that home-loading is very much second best, unless it's done on a big scale. I have learned, too, that you can become a bit of a bore as a specialist in loads and ammunition. I have a recollection of one man who carried his expertise to such an extent that he instructed his gunmaker to load his cartridges with No. 4's, but mark them as No. 6's on the top ward. He probably shot better in the secret enjoyment of his little trick.

If you yourself feel happier with a particular shot size, a particular loading, or a particular gun, you will shoot better. It is unscientific; but it is psychologically right.

12

How to Care for Your Guns

It would be salutory to assert that people who show the greatest punctiliousness in the care of their guns shoot the straightest. It wouldn't be true. It is undeniable that men who seem to have no respect for the condition of their weapons, like smokers who never clean their pipes, get satisfying results with them.

One reason is that a well-made gun can be subjected to abominable ill-treatment, and still give good service. The second more valid reason is the general adoption in recent years of cartridges with non-corrosive caps which, unlike the corrosive kind which induce rust in the barrels, are rust inhibitors. The new type of scrubbing wad is almost completely effective in eliminating the nuisance of leading deposited in the barrels. Theoretically, there is now no need to clean the barrels of a gun at all.

I can confirm the effectiveness of the now standard cartridges because I made the experiment—I hasten to add that it was with a weapon supplied to me for the purpose—of witholding the cleaning rod for an entire shooting season. When I finally overhauled the gun, the barrels came up free from blemish and moonbright. You can satisfy yourself on the matter in a few moments by firing a couple of rounds of the old corrosive cartridges—there are still plenty about—followed by two of the new sort. If you examine the barrels of the gun, before and after, you will find that the corrosive cartridges leave the barrels black with residue. The wads in the non-corrosive cartridges will clean out all that, leaving only flakes of waste in their wake.

The non-corrosive cartridge is an important advance; but what it can't eliminate is *atmospheric rusting.* While it is true that you can neglect gun-cleaning now to an extent which would be ruinous using corrosive caps, any man who values his gun, and the atmosphere affects the action as well as the insides of the barrels, is still inviting trouble if he doesn't clean at the end of a day's shooting as strictly as it was necessary when cartridge-fouling could corrode the barrels twenty-four hours after they were cold.

Anyhow, knowing how to clean guns properly is a useful part of the therapy to help you employ guns usefully in the field. Sheer familiarity with the working parts, the habit of handling them, the pleasure of making a fuss of them, will improve your shooting because, when you take one under your arm in the field, you will be in the company of a friend.

You will be familiar with its weight and its balance. You will take pride in the polish on the walnut stock, the glint on the thinly-oiled action plates and barrels. You will have achieved the prerequisite of all good shooting; that you are one with your gun.

Let the man who couldn't care less, and however straight his powder, go his own way. Gun care, even if it is not as necessary as it used to be, will make you a better shot.

Shooting in the days when the only powder was black powder (the stuff that is still used in fireworks and for blowing up the stumps of dead trees) was a messy business. Men came in from a day's sport with blackened

hands and faces, and the guns—perfumed like the
hangover of a pyrotechnic display—were best relegated
out of sight and smell. After forty rounds or so the
barrels were coked up like the bowl of a well-smoked
pipe. Your modern gun is, or should be, an ornament
which even the most fastidious female shouldn't object
to. I keep mine, as decorations, in a prominent position
in the house. But I take care that they are a credit to
me.

On your return home after a day in the field, however
tired you are, make a habit of dismounting your gun.
You may postpone cleaning it; but you shouldn't delay,
especially if it has been raining, in airing it in a dry
atmosphere. If the gun is still wet, give it a quick wipe
with a dry cloth, especially down the gutters on each
side of any double-barrelled gun with a raised rib. It is
one of the places where moisture commonly makes an
insidious entry through minute flaws and crevices in the
soldering to cause hidden *rusting* between the boards.

If it is a single-barrelled gun, a folding gun or a rifle,
open the breech. It also happens to be an extra insurance
that the gun is empty. But, in most cases, readers of this
book will be using conventional double game guns.

Up-end the barrels on a convenient shelf and put a
few drops of lubricating oil on each side of the rib,
starting at the bead, and leave the oil to penetrate to the
base. Then take the stock of the gun by the small of the
butt and give it a vigorous shake. If you have been in a
downpour, of the sort that wildfowlers are familiar with,
you will be surprised how many drops of rainwater you
can shake out through the striker holes in the action.
Place the stock butt upwards beside the barrels. After
that, it only takes a few moments; you can have your
bath with an easy conscience.

While you are in the tub, ask yourself whether you are
quite certain that you dismounted your gun correctly.

Oh yes, you reduced it to its three component parts. But far too many shooting men struggle with their weapons like blacksmith's apprentices.

Incidentally, when you are considering the purchase of a second-hand gun, it is a good tip to examine the lumps on the base of the barrels which hook into the action of the gun. If you find that the edges of the metal are bruised, or broken like old teeth, you will know that the owner of the gun, or at least one of its owners, has been a botcher. Just as well to look a little more carefully before you buy.

Mounting and dismounting the parts of a gun should be carried out as a drill. I was once told, before the age of two-pedal driving, that the secret of handling a car is to treat the clutch as if it were made of glass. You will do well to treat your gun as if it were made of glass, too.

What did you do when you dismounted your own gun? My guess is that you removed the forehand and placed it on the table beside you. You then twisted off the barrels and separated the three parts on the table. Right? All wrong.

The proper procedure is illustrated opposite page 82. You should do it like this. Tuck the gun under your arm in the ready position. With your left finger press the release button at the top of the forehand. Lift off the forehand, *and plant it in front of the loop on the barrels.* Still grasping the forehand on the loop, press open the lever of the action to its extremity with the pad of your right thumb, and keep it there. Now bend the barrels to a full right angle with the stock before you lift them off, as gently as if the barrels were made of glass. Put down the stock, and immediately replace the forehand on the barrels.

Assembling the gun, remove the forehand and again place it in front of the barrel loop. Holding the barrels perpendicularly, tuck the stock into the ready position under your arm. Make sure that your are pressing the action well home, and then slip the lumps into the action face. Lift the barrels to the stock, not the stock to the barrels. *This, of course, is the reverse of what you do when you are loading cartridges.* Complete the assembly of the gun by locking on the forehand.

Why all that? Without the grip that the forehand gives, barrels are inconvenient tubes to handle. The stock, without the barrels, is a stubby end-heavy object. By preserving a firm and comfortable grip on the barrels with the forehand, by using the pressure of your arm to hold the stock in position, you ensure that, when you bring the two together, you marry them at the correct angle to make an easy sucking fit.

Don't try and short circuit this process. The side lever must be at its full extension. The stock must be firmly squeezed under your arm. The lumps on the barrels of the gun must be introduced to the action from a complete right angle.

Master the drill, and you will find that friends with borrowed guns, and not enough knowledge of their working, will think that you are a wizard to be able to put their own guns together for them with such apparently casual ease.

Repeat: NEVER PULL THE TRIGGERS ON AN EMPTY SHOTGUN.

Putting a gun away, it seems the natural thing to do to release the pressure on the springs. Rifle shots are encouraged to do it. You can bust a shotgun jarring the action by pulling on empty chambers. The fact is that the main springs are always under tension. Inside the action, the difference between a cocked gun and an uncocked one is a difference in pressure of not more than a quarter of an inch. Put your gun away fully cocked. The springs won't mind; and, when you come to put the gun together again, you will find that you can assemble it more easily. In fact, unless you are experienced at the game, you are more likely to burr the lumps on the barrels if you have to twist them on against the pressure of the mainsprings.

Unless circumstances prevent it, never store a rifle or a shotgun in a case or a gunbag. The function of a case is to carry your weapon discreetly when you are making a journey. Guns left in a case for long periods, unless they are very carefully cocooned, deteriorate. The best place to keep a gun, even though it collects dust, is on an open rack. I can't even entirely recommend the glass-faced cases which were so fashionable in Victorian times for guns and books, too. They are airless containers which reek of the the specimen case. Guns, like unused cars in garages which are never opened, deteriorate. Guns like to be looked at, cosseted, and used.

The cleaning of guns, which used to be such a bind in the days of cartridges with corrosive primers, is now such a trifling chore in the expenditure of time and labor that it is the least of the problems of the contemporary shot. Time was when the shooting man was recommended to boil out his barrels, rifles and smooth-bored weapons, too, at regular intervals. You were warned not to leave a gun, more than a few hours after shooting, without scouring it.

The shooting man is spoiled today. The enemy is only humidity, rainwater, and, for the wildfowler, sea water. The inland shot, in good weather, can almost afford to be careless. But it's a bad habit, if you value your gun and take a personal pride in it. It is also precautionary to point out that, although non-corrosive cartridges have now been adopted as standard by the manufacturers, almost every gun cupboard and most country ironmongers are liable to have a remainder of old stock.

It is just as good as the new ammunition if it has been kept in a dry place, but its existence is an extra reason for watchful gun-cleaning. *Neglected fouling from one round of a corrosive cartridge can do just as much damage to the barrel of a gun as a hundred.*

One of the mysteries of what was called "The Mystery of Gunmakers" is that even the most expensive hand-made guns, presented in oak and leather cases, with brass corners and baize-lined interiors, are supplied with only the barest cleaning materials—a rod, a mop, a wire brush, and usually a prettily little square squat oil bottle which looks all right glittering in the case but, in use, is about the most inconvenient type of oil vessel which exists. Some of the very snootiest gun cases are provided with beautiful turnscrews with ebony handles for removing the lock plates. They offer a dangerous temptation because lock plates should never be removed except by a skilled hand. That's another tip if you are buying a second-hand gun. If the grooves in the screws of the lock plates are burred, it means that the action has been interfered with by someone who didn't know his business.

When you buy a gun, even if it is cased, you will need to provide adequate cleaning equipment for it yourself.

If you are a one gun man, a boxed cleaning outfit will be sufficient. But the fact that you are reading this book makes it likely that, over the years, you will acquire other weapons. Enthusiasts, who have the space, like to have their own gun-cleaning table with a miniature vice, with foam rubber or felt between the jaws, to hold the barrels for cleaning. Personally, I use a row of cleaning rods, nipped in a rack like billiards' cues, so that I haven't got to change the jags, brushes or mops for different processes. That is advanced practice, but it is advisable to begin against the day when you may have a gunroom of your own.

MODERN DOUBLE-BARRELLED 12-BORE GAME GUNS: *(Above)* A London-best sidelock gun. *(Below)* A boxlock. The hammerless sidelock, the most elegant-looking action, characterises the most expensive weapons. The boxlock, easily recognized by the squared-off action plate, is usually fitted to lower-priced guns. The boxlock, with its simple mechanism, is perhaps fractionally more reliable in hard service than the sidelock. Never buy a cheap sidelock.

ANTIQUE DOUBLE-BARRELLED 14-BORE MUZZLE LOADERS: The percussion gun *(Above)* which is primed on the nipples with copper caps, is the weapon which is most widely used by muzzle-loader enthusiasts. Flint guns *(Below)*, which remain safe to shoot, are rarer. It is dangerous to fire any antique arm without expert advice; and then with a reduced charge of black powder.

Professional gunmakers, with the traditional conservatism of their trade, use a twist of tow on a jag to clean out barrels. Don't imitate them. It calls for unusual skill to employ just the right amount of tow so that the cleaning rod doesn't jam. If you have to use a hammer to get the rod through the barrels—some people have—you can easily damage the tubes.

A tidy way to begin cleaning is to shove a knob of newspaper, which is soft and resilient, through the barrels, to remove flakes of fouling and to blot up damp. It isn't essential, but it will keep your other cleaning tools in better order.

Next, scour the barrels with a wire brush soaked with a mixture of Young's cleaner and three parts water—it is marketed under the trade name of Aquoil. It is not enough just to push the brush through. You must work it, trombone fashion, up and down a few inches at a time. It is the first half of the barrels which will need cleaning most thoroughly.

Dry out the barrels with a fitted patch on a split jag. Finish with a wool mop soaked in a mineral lubricant like Three-in-one or Express oil.

There are many variants in barrel-cleaning, many varieties of accessories, with which you can experiment. The principle is to wash, scour with a cleaner and rust preventor mixed with water (to eliminate the chloride), dry out, and lubricate with a thin film of mineral oil.

These days, you can get aerosol packs of oil to spray the accessories; but elbow grease behind the rod is still necessary.

Whenever you clean tubes, don't pass them without glimpsing down the barrels into the light *from both ends.* Look for the thin streaks of leading, the little marks that can subsequently do so much harm. Twisting the barrels in the light, you shouldn't be satisfied until you can't find a flaw in the surface.

Cleaning barrels is only part of the art of cleaning a gun. If yours is a self-ejecting model you should raise the extractors, and clean in and about them with an oily rag. It's surprising how much dirt they collect if they are not attended to. Give the extractors a touch of oil, just a touch. One of the best gunroom oilers is the fountain pen sort which ejects a spot of oil down a needle when you press it against a spring release. These oilers are ideal for fishing reels, too.

The forehand should be given a smear of oil in all its working parts. Oil, too, very slightly, in the cracks where the trigger blades extend from the action, the two pinholes in the face of the action, the lever mechanism, and safety catch. It is very important not to use oil freely in the working parts. It is essential to distinguish between Young's Cleaner, which has a sealing action against rust, and lubricants like Express and Three-in-One. The cleaner is for cleaning the barrels. Only the mineral oil should be used on the moving parts. If you use the wrong oil, or even overoil, you will eventually gum up the works.

If you get mud on the woodwork of your gun, you often will, the best way to get it out, without damaging the chequering, is with an old toothbrush. You can also polish the walnut stock with ordinary furniture polish or wax, made by Johnson's, especially for the purpose. It is worth doing if only because it is an added protection from warping caused by damp.

Wildfowlers, and people in the humidity of the tropics, need to be especially careful of these details. Sea air, and hot damp air, plays havoc with guns. The best protection is to keep the outer metal surfaces under a coat of Rangoon oil. If you have to put a gun away after shooting on the saltings, or in a tropical climate, make sure that you have a second and careful look at it within a few days. Warm damp and salt is as difficult to get rid of as the last rat in a barn.

Although you may care for your gun as thoroughly as I have suggested, there comes a time when guns, like cars, need expert servicing. Don't try and do it yourself. The gun trade is one which calls for an apprenticeship as long as a doctor's. Leave it to the craftsmen to regulate the action, the trigger pulls, the striker, and to advise about pits and dents in the barrels. The cost of cleaning and regulating, even in the most expensive gunshops, is reasonable. It is feckless not to use the service when you remember what a good gun costs.

I have said nothing directly about the care of miniature rifles. Normally, they are less vulnerable than shotguns. Any sportsman can take most of them to pieces, and put them together again. Cleaning them is simply a matter of modifying the instructions for cleaning shotguns. I have shot with a trombone-action .22 Browning for—oh dear!— over thirty years without its requiring any attention.

In range shooting, the enthusiasts are forever adjusting their sights and their trigger pulls, even rubbing their cartridges for greater accuracy. In the field, if you keep rust out of your gun, clean it and oil it at regular intervals; you will be unlucky if you have any real trouble in years of shooting. Even if the rifling becomes worn, you will still have a reasonable degree of accuracy over the short ranges at which the quarry is normally taken.

13

How to Approach Antique Arms

With the advent of breech-loaders in the latter half of the nineteenth century, the muzzle-loading guns of the sporting prints were relegated to the attic. As late as the thirties in this century, only a few enthusiasts had any use for them. You could pick up old arms in junk shops for as little as a few shillings. Not now.

Today, vintage guns are sought after like vintage cars; not only by arms collectors but by sportsmen who enjoy using them in the field. You can even buy replicas; and shooting by members of the Muzzle-Loaders Association is a regular feature of that festival of sport, the annual Game Fair of the County Landowners Association. So there may well come a time when you are tempted to try shooting with one yourself.

It is not a game to rush into as if it were a lark with a catapult. It calls for considerable gun knowledge and persnickety care. Smooth-bored muzzle-loaders shot just as far and as hard as modern shotguns. Muzzle-loading rifles were used by great hunters like Selous to kill elephants.

The hazard of personal accident and error to the man who is using them is much greater than it is with a breech-loader. The reason is that muzzle-loading guns are fired with *black powder,* which is devilishly combustible stuff. You can blow your hand off pouring a charge into a barrel in which a spark is still winking from the previous round. You can blow your head off if you look down the muzzles when you are pressing the ramrod home. You can burst the barrels, if, in error, you load a double charge.

The risk of a burst is far greater because a vintage muzzle-loader is almost certainly going to be a weapon over a hundred years old. The risk of metal fatigue is considerable.

My first advice to you, if you are keen enough to learn how the men who went shooting in top hats did it, is to seek the help of people in the know. The people in the know will tell you whether the gun you have got is safe, and the accessories you need. If you try to use the powder in a modern cartridge, you will blow yourself to smithereens.

But here is an introduction to the subject if only to prevent you from, on an impulse, making an ass of yourself; and possibly a mess of yourself.

If you acquire a vintage muzzle-loader, the very first precaution is to drop the ramrod down the barrel to ensure that a charge hasn't been left in the bottom of it. If the ramrod fails to ring on metal, take off the brass cap on the end of it, and strike in the worm screw it contains to draw the charge. If the job proves sticky, pour boiling water from a kettle down the tube. When you do it. make sure that you protect your hand with a thick cloth. Otherwise, you will find that the barrels are too hot to hold.

If you can't draw the charge with the hot water treatment, it may be necessary to remove the plugs in the base to clear it. In that event, it's gunsmith's work.

Whatever happens, even if there isn't a stale charge in the gun, boiling out the barrels is necessary. When the gun has dried, sluice it again with cold water from a bucket in the garden. Pump a rod with a wire brush and a wool mop until you force the water through the percussion nipples or, in the unlikely event that it's a flint-fired gun, through the touch hole. If the gun hasn't been used for a long time, you will be surprised at the amount of sooty water which squirts out at all points. You will be grateful, and so will the women of the house, that I told you to tackle the job with a bucket in the garden.

You must keep at it until the water you pump is quite clean. Next, apply boiling water again. It's the quick way of steaming the barrels dry.

Unlike a breech-loader, you can take off the lock-plate of a muzzle-loader by releasing a single screw. Carefully clean and lightly oil all the working parts. When the barrels are dry, oil them too. Then polish the stock. Most of the guns have woodwork which recovers a high polish in the most satisfactory way.

When you have sweetened your gun, don't dream of going into action with it without making a personal proof. Load it with only a nominal charge (more about that later) and lash it to the nearest convenient fence. Attach a long string to the trigger and don't pull the string until, as they warn you on fireworks, you have retired to a safe distance. If the gun stands a small charge, you can increase it. But make a thorough test that it is still sound before you put it to your shoulder.

The old gunmen had to deck themselves with accessories, the flint gunners even more than the ones with percussion weapons. The difference between them is that a flint gun, which was in use over a period of two hundred years, is fired by the sparks made by a wafer of flint striking an iron frizzen. The percussion gun, which had a comparatively brief history before the breech-loader was introduced, is primed with copper caps placed over hollow nipples, and fired like a cap pistol by the blow of a hammer. The guns which are used by muzzle-loader enthusiasts are nearly all percussion guns. The essential accessories are:

(1–2) A SHOT POUCH (made of leather) and a POWDER FLASK (usually copper or horn). Both have brass nozzles which can be adjusted to measure out the required charge. To use them, you turn them upside down with your forefinger placed over the nozzle, and spring slide releases which allow powder and shot to fill the chambers. In proper order, you pour the contents down the muzzle of the gun.

(3) You will need a supply of WADS to ram down the powder and shot. For the over-powder wad, greased felt is preferable. For the top-wad over the shot, screwed up bits of newspaper are excellent. When the gun is fired, the paper provides a satisfying display of pyrotechnics. In an emergency, you can just as well use dried grass.

(4) It is wise to carry a small SCREWDRIVER for running repairs, and essential to have a wire HAIRPIN for cleaning out the nipples of the gun when they coke up as they will.

Flint gun shooters also need a supply of Brandon flints, the Suffolk flints which were used by both sides at the Battle of Waterloo. The flints which are knapped today are generally rather soft, good for not much more than twelve shots. But, if you are fortunate enough to lay hands on the hard translucent toffee-colored ones favored by our forefathers, you can sometimes get forty shots from them before they splinter away.

Loading a muzzle-loader, it is a matter of sheer self-preservation to follow a rigorous drill:

(1) Place the butt of the gun against your boot, and push the muzzle away from you with a stiff arm in the stand-at-ease position.

(2) Draw out the ramrod from the rings under the barrels, and bounce the brass end on the plug in the

bases to ensure that the gun is empty. If it is a double-barrelled percussion weapon, as it probably will be, leave the rod in one barrel while you are loading the other. This is to prevent you putting in a double charge.
(3) Pour in a measure of black powder, and then tap the butt of the gun on the ground so that the powder settles evenly. But remember to keep the muzzles, in the stand easy position, pointing away from your head.
(4) Wad the powder down *firmly* with the rod. If it is loose, it is liable to squib ineffectively.
(5) Pour in the shot, and keep it from dribbing away, when you lift the gun, with a screw of newspaper. Don't tamp it down too tight on the shot.
(6) Raise the gun to the ready position, and draw back the hammers until they slip into half-cock. This is a catch which comes into operation before the mainsprings are fully compressed.
(7) Last, very much last, mount the copper percussion caps on the nipples of the gun. Don't raise the hammers to full cock until actually on the point of shooting.

If it is a flint gun, you raise the hammers to half-cock, open the frizzen, and prime the hollow pan adjacent to the touch-hole with a pinch of powder. Then lower the frizzen to keep the powder in position.

Unless you are a specialist, it is unlikely that you will shoot with a muzzle-loading rifle. However, the rules are the same. The difference is that you must learn to mould your own shot, the powder charge is much smaller and, with a well-fitting bullet in the rifling, you don't need wadding. Pea-rifles, as they used to be called, are comparable to present day miniatures. If you move into that class, you are unlikely to require advice from me.

Before you get anywhere near that class, rather while you are at the stage when you are inquisitively examining a muzzle-loader perhaps for the first time, don't mess about with the hammers. You can damage the action of a hammerless breach-loader, as I have already mentioned, by pulling the triggers on empty chambers. *If you release the hammers of a percussion gun on uncapped nipples, you will undoubtedly fracture them.* It will cost you, perhaps more than the price of the gun, to replace them. As long as there is a flint in the jaws of flint gun hammers, and the frizzen is down, you can spark them off on an empty gun without trouble. The resistance in the frizzen takes the shock off the hammer.

I am reluctant to give you more than a general guidance about loads. Even the sportsmen who shot with muzzle-loaders all their lives had diverging opinions; and they were shooting when the guns were new. The pressures developed by black powder *without a charge of lead on top* permit a wide margin of error. You can fire the stuff, the evidence is there on Guy Fawkes Night, in large quantities out of a paper tube. What happens when you place a charge of lead on top is what happens when you stamp your foot on a firecracker. The pressure makes a big difference to the bang.

The problem of loads is complicated because the right one not only varies with different calibres but with individual guns. A light load will reduce recoil and still maintain pellet density. As a mean, a 14-bore game gun of about 7 lb. weight should give a fairly reasonable killing pattern up to 45 yards with 1 oz. of shot and 2 3/4 to 3 drachmas of powder. You can easily measure the amounts because powder flasks and shot pouches are usually provided with two or three slots with which you set them for the amount of powder or shot your require.

The old gunmen sometimes recommended shot as large as No. 3 for partridge shooting. I recommend you stick to Nos. 6 or 7, and No. 4 for wildfowling. I also recommend you to under-charge an old gun. You will probably shoot just as well, and as far, as if at your peril you put it under the preloads. Modern powder and shot is anyhow far superior to the stuff our forefathers used.

You will have misfires. The usual reason is that the nipples of a percussion gun, or the touch-hole of a flint gun, get clogged with powder waste. This is where your hairpin comes in.

With muzzle-loaders, and black powder, careful cleaning especially of the nipples of percussion guns is vital to performance. Percussion guns are very liable to corrosion caused by the copper caps. Flint guns are free from it. But both need regular cleaning, scrubbing out would be a better phrase because they need cold water treatment like a small boy's ears, to get out the oily residue which collects heavily from black powder after about forty to fifty shots.

Before the development of muzzle-loading percussion guns, there was very little shooting at game on the wing. The reason, as you will readily appreciate after studying the method of straight shooting I am advocating, is that there is a time lag of about a 1/10th of a second, after pulling the trigger of a flint gun before it goes off. The flint has to strike the spark off the frizzen, the spark has to ignite the priming powder, and the priming powder explode the charge. If you are using a flint gun, and before you get used to it, it feels like half-an-hour before the mechanism moves into action.

One of the instructions which the old gunners emphasized to newcomers in the field was to overcome "flinching." Waiting for the gun to go off, novices turned away their heads, or even closed their eyes. There was even time for the quarry "to duck the charge." Because of the time lag flighting and driven-game shooting, as we know it today, was non-existent. Sportsmen were happy to stalk a sitting quarry, and to pull off shots at straight going away birds.

Colonel Peter Hawker, who wrote the classic work on

nineteenth-century shooting called *Instructions to Young Sportsmen,* is credited as the father of shooting on the wing. But, with a flint gun, I doubt very much if, famous shot in his time he was, he could pull down flighting pigeons the way a quite average shot, with a modern breech-loader, can now. His method of shooting partridges was to catch them by chasing them on a horse. After following a covey for several points, birds were so tired that he could dismount and knock them off when they were hardly fit to lift off the stubbles.

In an experimental mood. I have shot flying rooks with a flint gun. But it is a testing experience. The method is still to shoot on first aim, but to follow through with the gun, and eyes fixed on the target, for ten yards or more. If you can shoot one in ten that you would get with a breech-loader, you are not bad.

Percussion guns, on the contrary, are almost as efficient in action as modern breech-loaders. They take a lot of trouble to load, they are rather slower and generally heavier to handle; but, with a good push behind them, they can be used efficiently at fast-flying targets. Even Colonel Peter Hawker, who had fought with Wellington at the battle of Talavera in the Peninsular War, was converted to them in the end.

Your yourself may never shoot with muzzle-loaders. The barest knowledge of them will nevertheless be useful to you in handling modern arms. When you understand the disadvantages of trying to shoot straight a mere century ago, you will be better able to handle a modern gun with the ease and confidence it deserves.

14

Extras

A friend of mine, whom I introduced to salmon fishing, equipped himself with a new tackle so lavishly that, when we arrived on the water, he said, "Here I am, five hundred quid in my boots. What do I do next?" He was a famous man, a great shot as it happened, who made a first class fisherman. But his approach to a new sport was all wrong.

The temptation to invest in fal-lals and what-nots is common to all of us. The seductive appeal of Parker Hale's catalogue is sufficient to excite you to buy all manner of accessories you will never in practice use. My own gun cupboard is full of them.

Start light. With experience, you will learn what you really need in the way of gear. Try to be a skinflint until you have convinced yourself, under actual field conditions, what you really want. It varies with different people, and different circumstances.

As the purpose of this book is to teach straight safe shooting, what you don't want, however cold the weather, is full-fingered gloves. You cannot afford to restrict ease of movement on the triggers with a leathered finger. If it is too cold for you, don't shoot at all.

(1) The proper wear is a pair of shooting mitts with a

loop to ring over your trigger finger and woollen sleeves to keep your wrists warm. With warm wrists you won't have to bother about the circulation in your trigger finger. DON'T LOSE YOUR TOUCH.

(2) Whatever the weather, don't over clothe yourself. Wildfowlers, in particular, often do. Use a belt rather than braces, and wear the loosest jacket you can find. Robert Churchill, at his shooting school, kept a collection of jackets which hung on the shoulders as loose as robes. People were surprised how comfortably they shot in them.

(3) You gun should have a gun hand protector, made of spring steel covered in black morocco, which is slipped over the barrels like a sleeve, to extend the length of the forehand. On first appearance, you may wonder why it should come in useful. For the primary purpose for which it was designed you could almost certainly do without it.

It is called a protector because it insulates the aiming hand from barrels which become overheated from constant shooting—a problem which is unlikely to bother anyone except a man shooting non-stop with two guns and a loader. In practice, the best protection it normally gives is in wintry weather when the barrels are *too cold* to handle with comfort.

But I recommend the use of a gun sleeve for the same reason that I favor a rifle with plenty of wood under the barrel. It extends the grip on the forehand, and makes for more comfortable handling. Some shotguns, relatively few in this country, are made with what is called a beaver-tailed forehand which provides a full and rounded shape. Most shotguns, even the very best, have forehands which, although they look good, feel starved. With a gun that fits you, you will find that the flesh between forefinger and thumb presses on the forehand release button. A gun sleeve fills the cavity. It is a cheap accessory which will aid your gunmounting. It will be the more valuable in helping you to regulate your grip if your gun happens to be a bit short in the stock for you.

If you can afford the best, you can have a sleeve which locks into position on the barrels on the gun. If you use the sort that simply springs on to the barrels, a minor snag is that the sleeve tends to slip on recoil. But it is really no trouble to pull it tight again as you recover a ready position.

(4) If recoil worries you, a rubber butt shoe which you can slip on or off like the barrel sleeve, is not to be discounted. If your stock is on the short side, it is also an economic way of slightly increasing length.

(5) If the noise of other people shooting nearby distracts you, try rubber earplugs until familiarity breeds contempt.

(6) I have referred in the drill to snap caps. Simply, they are dummy metal tubes with spring loaded horn buttons which you can load into the barrels of a gun when you want to exercise the trigger springs, or test the ejector mechanism. In expensive gun cases they are often provided as an accessory. They have no use except to prevent your jarring the action by pulling the trigger on empty chambers. The gun won't benefit from their use. You, in dry practice, may find them helpful. They are reasonably-priced; and, if you like pulling triggers for the hell of it, they are an insurance against damaging your gun.

(7) Shooting all my life, I have arrived at the conclusion that the best place to carry cartridges is the side pocket of the jacket. By all means have a cartridge bag. The type of pigskin bag, with a metal oval to keep the mouth open, designed by Payne-Gallway, the famous Victorian shot, has never been improved on. But even a fifty-round bag slung over the shoulder restricts freedom of movement. At a stand, I drop mine on the ground, and

draw from it only to replenish my pocket.

Many shots use cartridge belts, or bandoliers. Contemporary shooting coats are fitted with cartridge recesses. But I fancy that loading is a little slower with artificial aids than it is from the pocket. It is a matter on which you must suit your own taste.

(8) Certainly equip yourself with a pocket cartridge extractor, especially if you are using a non-ejecting gun, or shooting wildfowl in wintry conditions in which cartridges are liable to swell.

(9) For wildfowling or pigeon-shooting it is a second investment to buy a mask with open eyeholes to shield the white of your face. Otherwise, a hat is essential. For pheasant-shooting, a bare head won't turn the birds. For partridge and grouse-shooting (if you have the luck to enjoy it) a hat is required wear to prevent birds jinking. A mask, or mud on your face, is an advantage in wildfowling. A mask for pigeon-shooting is worth a lot to the total bag.

(10) One of the first luxuries I recommend you to buy is a sheepskin-lined gunbag. They are expensive, but guns cost so much today that it is mere prudence to carry them about in a bag in which the chances of barrel dents are materially reduced.

15

Conclusion

Extract from the Report of the Government Committee on Cruelty to Wild Animals (1951):

The shooting of wild animals of all kinds is very widely practiced both as a method of control and for sport. If the animal fired at were always killed outright, shooting would be one of the most humane methods of control, but this is by no means always the case and there can be no doubt that it may involve great suffering if the animal is wounded and escapes, particularly if it is not followed up and killed. This happens less frequently with experienced shots, but we think that a great deal of shooting is done by people who lack the necessary skill and experience. Despite the high cost of cartridges, many people who lack the necessary skill are accustomed to try their hand with a gun from time to time, and there is a tendency for these people, and also for some who shoot more frequently, to fire at too great a range or to use the wrong type of cartridge. At present anyone who takes out a gun license can use a gun no matter how unskilled he may be, and some witnesses have suggested that nobody should be allowed to shoot until he has passed the shooting test. This suggestion is in our view impractical.

Most of the opponents of field sports advocate shooting as an alternative method of control and consider it to be more

124

satisfactory and more humane than hunting or any other method. We agree that, in many circumstances, shooting is a very important valuable method of controlling a number of animals such as the fox, but at the same time we are convinced that for the reasons we have given inexpert shooting causes a great deal of unnecessary suffering. Also we do not accept the view which was expressed to us by some witnesses that a normal animal does not normally suffer from its wounds to any appreciable extent... We realize, however, that shooting is a convenient method of control on which farmers, gamekeepers and others concerned with the control of pests depend to a great extent. It is a common practice for farmers to walk round their land with a gun and to shoot any rabbits or other pests as the opportunity arises, and this helps considerably to keep the land free from pests and consequently to safeguard food. Because of this it is clearly contrary to the national interest for us to recommend that shooting should be prohibited, nor has any witness proposed this. As it would be quite impossible to attempt to regulate shooting by laying down minimum ranges and other details of that sort, there is no recommendation for legislation that we can usefully make, but we think that more should be done to instruct people in the use of guns.

At the end of this manual, its aim to assist in fulfilling the recommendations of the Government Committee, I hope you recognize the essential fallacy in the official conclusion. It assumes that the people who wound animals are those "who lack the necessary skill and experience." But, as I have shown, novices who don't know the drill are unlikely to hurt anything except their own jaws, and the only real risk is for the people who are unfortunate enough to be out with them. The man who wounds, without making a clean kill, is the experienced shot who is "off his day."

The difference between a clean kill and a tailed bird is a matter of feet. In the swing of the barrels of the gun, it is a measure of inches. It happens for the familiar reasons that (1) the gun tries to make too sure, (2) there is a fractional hesitation in trigger-pressing, (3) footwork is off-balance.

There is no definitive solution to the problem because human error, in shooting as in every other activity, is ineradicable.

Unfortunately, the risk of wounding without killing is far greater when game is walked-up, the average man's sport, than it is when it is driven over the guns by a line of beaters. You are more likely to kill clean shooting heads than tails.

Not the least of the problems is that hard-hit birds, even hares, can go on, and leave you with the impression that you have missed. On big shoots it is customary to station pickers-up a quarter of a mile behind the line. In partridge drives in particular, ten per cent of the bag, is often picked behind. On big shoots, the gamekeepers go out the following morning searching for lost birds, and runners.

In you own case, shooting as you often will be on your own, my advice is that you keep your eyes skinned for *a wince.* If you see that fractional movement, your responsibility is to go after the bird you have shot at. If you fire at a hare, and she stops at intervals as she goes away, she is wounded. Go after her.

Woodpigeons are more tricky. Their natural flight is a wincing one. They can drop feathers when they haven't been touched. Only sheer experience can tell you when you ought to go after them.

The nearest I can get to a humane answer is to tell you that every keen shooting man ought to have a working dog. He may not be a good dog—good dogs are as rare as good masters—but a dog uses his nose as we use our eyesight. He lives in a world of delicious and subtle blocks of smell. If you guide him on eyesight to the point where you yourself are blind, his nose will find things you couldn't possibly find out for yourself.

I started this book by writing that any proper man is fascinated by the glint of gunmetal. Here, I remind you that no man could appear more contemptible than one who believes that the handling of guns is something which comes naturally; that the quarry he shoots at doesn't matter; that he can shoot anyway.

Shooting is a proud man's business. For results, it calls for personal discipline, controlled confidence, a humane respect for the animals, and a deep sense of responsibility for the lethal weapons in one's hands.

Over to you, son . . .

Appendix

BORES OF GUN

Description	Approximate Shot Charge oz.	Approximate Weight of Gun lb.
4-bore 4 in.	3–4	$14\frac{1}{2}$–$16\frac{1}{2}$
8-bore $3\frac{1}{4}$ in.	2–$2\frac{1}{2}$	$10\frac{1}{2}$–$12\frac{1}{2}$
10-bore $2\frac{7}{8}$ in.	$1\frac{7}{16}$–$1\frac{5}{8}$	8–9
10-bore $2\frac{5}{8}$ in.	$1\frac{1}{4}$–$1\frac{3}{4}$	$7\frac{1}{2}$–8
12-bore 3 in.*	$1\frac{3}{8}$–$1\frac{1}{2}$	$7\frac{3}{4}$–$8\frac{1}{2}$
12-bore $2\frac{3}{4}$ in.*	$1\frac{1}{4}$	$7\frac{1}{2}$–$7\frac{3}{4}$
12-bore $2\frac{1}{2}$ in.*	1–$1\frac{1}{8}$	$6\frac{1}{2}$–7
16-bore $2\frac{3}{4}$ in.	1–$1\frac{1}{16}$	$6\frac{1}{2}$
16-bore $2\frac{1}{2}$ in.	$\frac{7}{8}$–$\frac{15}{16}$	$5\frac{3}{4}$–6
20-bore $2\frac{3}{4}$ in.	$\frac{7}{8}$–$\frac{15}{16}$	$5\frac{3}{4}$–6
20-bore $2\frac{1}{2}$ in.	$\frac{3}{4}$–$\frac{13}{16}$	$5\frac{1}{2}$
24-bore $2\frac{1}{2}$ in.	$\frac{11}{16}$	5
28-bore $2\frac{1}{2}$ in.	$\frac{5}{8}$	$4\frac{3}{4}$
32-bore $2\frac{1}{2}$ in.	$\frac{1}{2}$	4
.410-bore $2\frac{1}{2}$ in.	$\frac{7}{16}$	$3\frac{3}{4}$

PELLETS IN GAME CHARGES

oz. of Shot	Size of Shot			
	4	5	6	7
$1\frac{1}{2}$	255	330	408	510
$1\frac{7}{16}$	244	316	391	489
$1\frac{3}{8}$	234	303	374	468
$1\frac{5}{16}$	223	289	357	446
$1\frac{1}{4}$	213	275	340	425
$1\frac{3}{16}$	202	261	323	404
$1\frac{1}{8}$	191	248	306	383
$1\frac{1}{16}$	181	234	289	361
1	170	220	272	340
$\frac{15}{16}$	159	206	255	319
$\frac{7}{8}$	149	193	238	298
$\frac{13}{16}$	138	179	221	276
$\frac{3}{4}$	128	165	204	255
$\frac{11}{16}$	117	151	187	234
$\frac{5}{8}$	106	138	170	212
$\frac{9}{16}$	96	124	153	191
$\frac{1}{2}$	85	110	136	170

* Churchill 'XXV' guns with 25-in. barrels are built approximately 8 oz. lighter

TRUE CYLINDER (= 40 PER CENT) PATTERNS

oz. of Shot	Pellets in 30-in. circle at 40 YARDS for different SIZES of Shot			
	4	5	6	7
$1\frac{1}{2}$	102	132	163	204
$1\frac{3}{8}$	94	121	150	187
$1\frac{1}{4}$	85	110	136	170
$1\frac{1}{8}$	76	99	122	153
$1\frac{1}{16}$	72	94	116	144
1	68	88	109	136
$\frac{7}{8}$	60	77	95	119
$\frac{3}{4}$	51	66	82	102
$\frac{11}{16}$	47	60	75	94
$\frac{5}{8}$	42	55	68	85
$\frac{9}{16}$	38	50	61	76
$\frac{1}{2}$	34	44	54	68

IMPROVED CYLINDER (= 50 PER CENT) PATTERNS

oz. of Shot	Pellets in 30-in. circle at 40 YARDS for different SIZES of Shot			
	4	5	6	7
$1\frac{1}{2}$	128	165	204	255
$1\frac{7}{16}$	122	158	196	245
$1\frac{3}{8}$	117	152	187	234
$1\frac{5}{16}$	111	145	179	223
$1\frac{1}{4}$	107	138	170	213
$1\frac{3}{16}$	101	131	162	202
$1\frac{1}{8}$	96	124	153	192
$1\frac{1}{16}$	91	117	145	181
1	85	110	136	170
$\frac{15}{16}$	80	103	128	160
$\frac{7}{8}$	75	97	119	149
$\frac{13}{16}$	69	90	111	138
$\frac{3}{4}$	64	83	102	128
$\frac{11}{16}$	59	76	94	117
$\frac{5}{8}$	53	69	85	106
$\frac{9}{16}$	48	62	77	96
$\frac{1}{2}$	43	55	68	85

HALF CHOKE (= 60 PER CENT) PATTERNS

oz. of Shot	Pellets in 30-in. circle at 40 YARDS for different SIZES of Shot			
	4	5	6	7
$1\frac{1}{2}$	153	198	244	306
$1\frac{7}{16}$	146	190	235	293
$1\frac{3}{8}$	140	182	224	280
$1\frac{5}{16}$	134	174	214	267
$1\frac{1}{4}$	128	165	204	255
$1\frac{3}{16}$	121	157	194	242
$1\frac{1}{8}$	115	148	148	230
$1\frac{1}{16}$	109	140	173	217
1	102	132	163	204
$\frac{15}{16}$	95	124	153	191
$\frac{7}{8}$	89	116	143	179
$\frac{13}{16}$	83	108	133	166
$\frac{3}{4}$	77	99	122	153
$\frac{11}{16}$	70	91	112	140
$\frac{5}{8}$	64	82	102	127
$\frac{9}{16}$	58	74	92	115
$\frac{1}{2}$	51	66	81	102

FULL CHOKE (= 70 PER CENT) PATTERNS

oz. of Shot	Pellets in 30-in. circle at 40 YARDS for different SIZES of Shot			
	4	5	6	7
$1\frac{1}{2}$	178	231	285	357
$1\frac{7}{16}$	170	221	274	342
$1\frac{3}{8}$	163	212	261	328
$1\frac{5}{16}$	156	202	249	312
$1\frac{1}{4}$	149	192	238	298
$1\frac{3}{16}$	142	183	226	283
$1\frac{1}{8}$	134	174	214	268
$1\frac{1}{16}$	127	164	202	253
1	119	154	190	238
$\frac{15}{16}$	112	144	179	223
$\frac{7}{8}$	105	135	167	209
$\frac{13}{16}$	97	125	155	194
$\frac{3}{4}$	90	115	143	179
$\frac{11}{16}$	82	106	131	163
$\frac{5}{8}$	75	97	119	148
$\frac{9}{16}$	67	86	107	134
$\frac{1}{2}$	59	77	95	119

Index

131